World Airline Colours

Volume One
Completely updated edition

By: Ricky-Dene Halliday

Aviation Data Centre
London • England

Published by:
The Aviation Data Centre Ltd.
PO Box 92, Feltham,
Middlesex TW13 4SA, England

Telephone/Fax: (0181) 751-3317

Distributed in the USA by:
World Transport Press, Inc.
PO Box 521238, Miami,
Florida 33152-1238, USA

Telephone: (305) 477-7163
Fax: (305) 599-1995

Origination and Printing by:
Paul Bennett & Associates,
No.5 The Grand Union Business Park,
Packet Boat Lane, Cowley,
Middlesex UB8 2GH, England

Telephone: (01895) 846409
Fax: (01895) 850144

ISBN: 0 946141 51 7

INTRODUCTION

World Airline Colours was originally the title given to a series of four books published by the Aviation Data Centre/Browcom Publishing between 1985 and 1987, collectively detailing the liveries of nearly 600 airlines. Compiled by Nigel M. Tomkins, these became a standard source of reference in airline recognition, covering the liveries and equipment of the mid to late 1980s with uncompromising accuracy and attention to detail.

This volume is the first of the original four to be updated and includes many airlines and liveries which are totally new to the series. It has been published in the established A5 casebound format and features 148 of the world's major international airlines.

For further information regarding the World Airline Colours series and other titles published by the Aviation Data Centre, including World Airline Colours of Yesteryear, Airlines & Airliners and World Airline Fleets News, please write to: The Aviation Data Centre Ltd, PO Box 92, Feltham, Middlesex TW13 4SA, England.

ILLUSTRATIONS:

Mike Baker - Air Transat, Air Ukraine, El Al, FedEx, Lufthansa; **Charles Bargibant** - Sabena; **Luc Bereni** - Royal Airlines; **Dario Cocco** - Air Inter; **Peter J. Cooper** - American Trans Air; **Dave Howell** - Syrianair; **Bill Hough** - Aeroflot; **Stephane Mutzenburg** - Air Mauritius; **Ton Jochems** - Air UK, Transavia, Vnukovo Airlines; **Stuart Kaye** - Air Belgium; **Christian Laugier** - Air Algerie, Air Charter, Air France, Air Liberte, AOM French Airlines, Aviaco, Olympic Airways, Tunis Air; **Flemming Lovenvig** - SAS; **J.M. Magendie/Avimage** - PIA; **Nick Mills** - Martinair; **Malcolm Nason** - Air 2000; **Piotr Pasnicki** - AZAL; **Maurice Patrick** - Excalibur Airways; **Augusto Gomez Rojas** - Cubana; **SPA Photography** - Virgin Atlantic; **Michael Steinlein** - Sobelair; **Shingo Takahashi** - Air China, All Nippon Airways, Canadian Airlines Intl., Cathay Pacific, Delta Air Lines, Northwest, Thai Airways Intl; **Peter Tancred** - Latavio; **Richard Vandervord** - Air Europa, Air India, Air New Zealand, Air UK Leisure, Air Zimbabwe, African Safari Airways, Belavia, Braathens SAFE, British World, Caledonian Airways, Continental Airlines, Crossair, Garuda Indonesia, Iberia, Icelandair, Maersk Air, Meridiana, Monarch Airlines, Transaero, Viasa, World Airways; **Diego Ruiz de Vargas** - Air Liberte Tunisie, Air Seychelles, KLM, Luxair, Premiair, Spanair; **Rolf Wallner** - EVA Airways, Korean Air, Palair Macedonian, Swissair; **Marcel Walther** - Aerolineas Argentinas, Air Afrique, Air China, Air Columbus, Air Lanka, Airtours, American Airlines, Condor, Egyptair, Emirates, Finnair, GB Airways, Hapag Lloyd, JAL, Lauda Air, Onur Air, Philippine Airlines, Royal Nepal Airlines, TAP Air Portugal, TMA, Turkmenistan Airlines, TWA, USAir and Viva Air.

ADRIA AIRWAYS

Adria Airways is the Republic of Slovenia's principle carrier, providing regular scheduled services from Ljubljana to Frankfurt, Istanbul, London, Manchester, Maribor (Slovenia), Moscow, Munich, Paris, Rome, Skopje (Macedonia), Split (Croatia), Tirana, Vienna and Zurich. The airline was formed in 1968 as the successor to the original Adria Airways and until May 1986 was known as Inex Adria Airways.

The airline is equipped with two De Havilland Canada Dash 7 turboprops, three McDonnell Douglas DC-9-30s, five MD-80s and three Airbus Industrie A320-200s, the size of the fleet reflecting Adria's now dormant role as a leading holiday charter airline. Surplus capacity is regularly leased to other carriers and Adria Airways has been successful in placing its entire MD-80 and A320 fleets during the peak summer months, leaving the Dash 7s and DC-9-30s to cover the modest scheduled network from Ljubljana.

The livery illustrated by Airbus Industrie A320-231 S5-AAC was introduced by Adria Airways to replace the previous Inex Adria image and has, at some time, been displayed by all types currently operated. The colour combination represents blue skies and the turquoise waters of the Adriatic, an image clearly designed with the holidaymaker in mind. The MD-80 and A320 aircraft may at times appear in hybrid liveries between lease contracts, and at least one MD-80 still wears remnants of the previous Inex Adria design.

AER LINGUS

Aer Lingus operates a modern all-jet fleet on services connecting the Irish Republic with cities in the United Kingdom, Europe and the United States. Domestic and regional services are the responsibility of a separate division, which flies Saab 340Bs and Fokker 50s under the name of Aer Lingus Commuter.

Short to medium haul flights are operated by six Boeing 737-400s and ten 737-500s and connect Dublin with Amsterdam, Birmingham, Brussels, Copenhagen, Cork, Dusseldorf, Frankfurt, London, Manchester, Milan, Paris, Rome and Zurich on a scheduled basis. Direct flights also link Cork and Shannon with London. In addition, the domestic and regional network of Aer Lingus Commuter provides service to East Midlands, Edinburgh, Glasgow, Leeds/Bradford and Newcastle, as well as connecting Connaught, Cork, Dublin, Kerry County, Galway and Shannon domestically. During the summer of 1994 Aer Lingus introduced three new 331-seat Airbus Industrie A330s on its long haul transatlantic routes to New York and Boston, replacing Boeing 747-100 equipment that has been in use since 1970. The carrier is also credited with two Boeing 767-300/ERs, but these aircraft are generally leased to other carriers.

The traditional Shamrock motif has survived many livery changes and will no doubt continue to so as and when Aer Lingus eventually looks to update its image. Created by design consultants King and Wetherell and illustrated by Airbus Industrie A330-301 EI-DUB, the livery is both distinctive and colourful and emphasises the carrier's Irish identity extremely well. The Fokker 50s and Saab 340Bs wear the standard two-tone green and blue colouring but with 'Aer Lingus Commuter' titles.

AEROFLOT-RUSSIAN INTERNATIONAL AIRLINES

Aeroflot-Russian International Airlines is the surviving element of the former state-owned Soviet national carrier, known simply as Aeroflot. The airline is responsible for passenger and freight services connecting cities such as Moscow and St. Petersburg with points throughout the CIS, Europe, Africa, Asia, Europe, the Middle and Far East, North, Central and South America and the Caribbean.

A large fleet includes Ilyushin Il-62s, Ilyushin Il-76s, Il-86s, Il-96-300s, Tupolev Tu-134s and Tu-154s, with Tu-204s on order. In addition, the airline is also equipped with four Airbus Industrie A310-300s and two Boeing 767-300/ERs, the latter added during the summer of 1994 for use on nonstop services to North America.

Most aircraft continue to display the previous Aeroflot image but with a Russian flag, complete with grey highlights, replacing that of the former Soviet Union. In its complete form the tail is painted grey overall, as illustrated by Il-86 RA-86113. A modern red, white and blue livery remains synonymous to the small Airbus A310-300 fleet. Designed by the manufacturer, it features broken lines of red in varying widths beneath solid blue tail colouring. However, the use of a double sided Eagle motif sparked some controversy when first unveiled and it is therefore unlikely to be adopted fleetwide.

AEROLINEAS ARGENTINAS

The flag carrier of the South American republic of Argentina was formed in 1949 and has expanded to the point where it now flies to North and South America, Europe and Australasia, as well as providing numerous domestic flights to destinations within Argentina.

A fleet of six Boeing 747-200Bs is kept busy on routes connecting the capital, Buenos Aires, with Auckland, Frankfurt, Lima, London, Los Angeles, Madrid, Miami, Montreal, New York, Paris, Rio de Janeiro, Rome and Sydney. The airline has recently added three ex-Delta Airbus A310-300s to supplement or replace the larger '747s on routes to North America. Domestically, the airline generally uses three Fokker F.28 Fellowships, one McDonnell Douglas MD-83 and ten Boeing 737-200s, but other types also figure on some higher density sectors. A fleet of eight Boeing 727-200s and six MD-88s provide service between Buenos Aires and other major cities within South America, including Asuncion, Bogota, Caracas, Florianopolis, Guayaquil, La Paz, Lima, Panama/Balboa and Rio de Janeiro, in addition to supplementing the domestic fleet.

All fleet members wear the livery illustrated by Boeing 747-287B LV-MLR. The design features twin cheatlines of medium and dark blue, which extend from the nose, widen along the fuselage and finally terminate on the fin, where each is topped by a similarly coloured 'A' initial. Dark blue 'Aerolineas Argentinas' titles are carried on the forward fuselage together with the traditional bird logo, which has now become a secondary feature of the design.

ADRIA
AIRBUS A320

Aer Lingus

RA-86113
АЭРОФЛОТ

AEROLINEAS ARGENTINAS
LV-MLR

AIR AFRIQUE

Air Afrique was formed in March 1961 as a multi-national venture with the involvement of Cameroon, the Central African Republic, Chad, Congo-Brazzaville, Dahomey, Gabon, the Ivory Coast, Mauritania, Niger, Senegal and Upper Volta, to pool the resources of each nation for the funding of an international airline. The organisation has changed over the years with some countries joining and others leaving to create their own independent national carriers. Today, Air Afrique provides regional scheduled passenger and freight services throughout Central and West Africa and northerly to Europe (France, Italy and the United Kingdom) and North Africa. In addition, a thrice-weekly service is also flown to New York.

Three McDonnell Douglas DC-10-30s are used on the mainline international services to New York, Marseille and Paris. A leased Boeing 737-300 is employed on thinner regional routes, which otherwise are the responsibility of three Airbus Industrie A300B4s and five A310-300s. The A310s are also used on routes to Bordeaux, Lyon and Rome, with Marseille and Paris being served by both Airbus types operated. Air Afrique also uses leased Antonov An-12 and Boeing 707 equipment for its all-cargo operations.

With so many nationalities involved, it was logical that Air Afrique's livery, illustrated by Airbus A300B4-203 TU-TAT, should make use of neutral colours, and consequently bright shades of emerald and lime green were chosen to colour the broad cheatlines. The livery's centrepiece is unquestionably the ethnic tail logo, which symbolises far reaching services by the use of a Gazelle's head spanning a stylised globe.

AIR ALGERIE

Air Algerie was originally formed in 1946 as CGTA and adopted its present title in April 1953, when Compagnie Air Transport was absorbed. Today, the state-owned airline serves the African capitals of Bamako, Cairo, Casablanca, Dakar, Niamey, Nouakchott, Ouagadougou and Tunis; the European cities of Barcelona, Berlin, Brussels, Frankfurt, Geneva, Lille, London, Lyon, Madrid, Marseille, Moscow, Nice, Paris, Prague, Rome, Sofia, Toulouse, Warsaw and Zurich; and Beirut and Damascus in the Middle East. In addition, the airline also maintains a comprehensive domestic network, serving over twenty-five points from the capital, Algiers.

Most domestic and international services are flown with Boeing 727-200s and 737-200s, of which eleven and sixteen respectively are employed. A small fleet of Fokker Friendships connect communities which are unable to support jet service, in addition to supplementing the smaller Boeing 737s at off peak times. Additional capacity is provided by four Airbus Industrie A310-200s and three Boeing 767-300s, which feature on domestic and international trunk routes, primarily to points in France. Two Lockheed L.100-30 Hercules freighters are also operated by the carrier.

The livery illustrated by Lockheed L.100-30 Hercules 7T-VHK was introduced by Air Algerie during the summer of 1982, basically as a modified version of an earlier design. The key feature is the red tail motif, which is thought to represent the Arabic equivalent of the company's 'AH' flight prefix, whilst also resembling a bird in flight. The national colours of red, white and green adorn the fuselage with titles appearing in English and Arabic respectively. It should also be noted that two of the four Airbus A310-200s are operated in basic Libyan Arab markings, on lease.

AIR BELGIUM

Air Belgium was formed on May 3rd 1979 as Abelag Airways and adopted its present title the following year. Operating mostly on behalf of its major shareholder, Sun International, the company provides charter flights to popular holiday destinations in Europe, the Mediterranean area and Florida.

A modest but hard working fleet currently includes one Boeing 737-400 and one 757, the latter delivered new to the carrier in October 1989.

Air Belgium's livery, illustrated by Boeing 757-23A OO-ILI, successfully promotes a holiday airline image whilst also employing the red, yellow and black colouring of the national flag. A bright yellow windowline flows along the fuselage and up the fin's leading edge, accompanied by a broader band of red. White 'AB' initials are displayed over the red backdrop of the fin, with 'Air Belgium' titles appearing in black uppercase lettering on the cabin roof.

AIR CANADA

Air Canada has existed since April 10th 1937 when it was formed as Trans Canada Airlines, the present title being adopted during 1964. As Canada's foremost international carrier, the company provides scheduled passenger services to points in Europe, Asia, the United States and the Caribbean, as well as maintaining an extensive domestic route network.
Domestic and regional flights are operated by a vast fleet of McDonnell Douglas DC-9-30s and Airbus Industrie A320-200s, with Boeing 767-200s providing additional capacity on high density routes within Canada and to the United States. Many Boeing 767-200s have been configured for transatlantic operations, providing service from Calgary, Edmonton, Halifax, Montreal, Ottawa, St. Johns, Toronto and Vancouver. Additional long-haul capacity is provided by a mixed fleet of Boeing 747s, including three of the latest series -400 model, which feature on the mainline international routes. Three Lockheed TriStars (retired in October 1990) and a Boeing 767-300 (previously leased out) have also been pressed into domestic and international service in recent times. In addition, twenty-five A319s, ten Canadair Regional Jets, five Boeing 767-300/ERs and six A340-300s are on order.

The livery illustrated by Boeing 747-433 C-GAGN was unveiled on December 1st 1993 to supersede a design that, despite various modifications through the years, had remained basically unchanged since Air Canada's birth in 1964. The new image uses a highly effective combination of autumn red and dark green, with a natural Maple Leaf as its centrepiece. For the sentimentalists, the original motif can still be found alongside bold 'Air Canada' titles, which appear in a new upper case style, as the only remaining link with the post TCA design. The natural look is complimented by a 'snowy' white fuselage, which replaces the previous red and burgundy cheatline arrangement and grey underside colouring. The new image is also being adopted by Air Canada's commuter affiliates, which include Air Alliance, Air BC, Air Nova, Air Ontario, Air Toronto and NWT Air.

AIR AFRIQUE
TU-TAT

7T-VHK
CARGO
ALGERIE
الخطوط الجوية الجزائرية

AIR BELGIUM
AB
OO-ILI

AIR CANADA

AIR CHARTER

Air Charter was formed on February 7th 1966 as a wholly-owned charter subsidiary of Air France, and began operations using aircraft loaned from its parent soon afterwards. In 1970 the airline purchased its own fleet of Caravelle IIIs from Air France and these were joined in 1972 by two ex-PSA Boeing 727-200s, which had been acquired to perform non-stop flights from Paris to the Canary Islands and the southern tip of Morocco with a full payload. Today, the airline flies from over thirty French provincial cities and with the ongoing support of Air France is well equipped to offer holiday flights and ad-hoc charters to destinations in Europe, the Middle East, North Africa and North America. Since 1978, ownership has been shared between Air France (80%) and Air Inter (20%).

Aircraft are leased from Air France or Euralair as required, with equipment currently assigned to Air Charter including three Boeing 737-200s, one 737-500, two Airbus Industrie A320-200s and two widebodied A300B4s.

A simple but extremely effective livery, illustrated by Airbus Industrie A320-211 F-GLGE, features a patriotic red, white and blue streamer, which starts immediately after red Air Charter titles and ultimately fans out to colour the fin. The fuselage is otherwise painted white overall to facilitate the interchange of aircraft with Air France.

AIR CHINA

Air China was created on July 1st 1988 to succeed the Beijing-based operation of the Civil Aviation Administration of China (CAAC), which had been responsible for all airline services since 1949. By far the largest international carrier to emerge following the decentralisation of the Chinese airline industry, Air China now offers services connecting Beijing and other Chinese cities with points in Africa, Australasia, Europe, the Middle and Far East and North America. The carrier also connects more than thirty destinations within China, including the major cities of Chengdu, Guangzhou, Harbin, Shanghai, Wuhan and Xian.

For domestic and regional operations, Air China is equipped with six locally built Yunshuji Y-7s (An-24s), four British Aerospace 146-100s, three Boeing 737-200s and seventeen 737-300s. Medium to long haul capacity is provided by two Boeing 707-320Cs, six 767-200/ERs, four 767-300s, four Boeing 747SPs, three 747-200Bs and eight 747-400s. For cargo-only flights, Air China has acquired a purpose built Boeing 747-200F freighter and two Lockheed L.100-30s.

Air China's livery, illustrated by Boeing 747-4J6 B-2458, is based on the previous blue and white colouring of CAAC. A white cabin roof and grey painted underside are neatly separated by twin medium blue cheatlines of different width. The Chinese flag, the focal point of the previous CAAC image, now appears on the forward cabin roof alongside black Air China titles - which are also displayed in Chinese. The tail motif is in the form of a stylised red phoenix, known locally as a symbol of good fortune, and also appears on the winglets of the 747-400s.

AIR CLUB INTERNATIONAL

Air Club International commenced operations on June 15th 1994, having been formed during the previous year to serve popular international holiday destinations on a seasonal charter basis. During its first summer the airline flew from Vancouver to London (Gatwick), Manchester, Glasgow, Belfast, Frankfurt and Amsterdam, and from Toronto to Barcelona, Lyon, Marseille, Nice, Paris and Toulouse. During the winter months it will focus mainly on holiday destinations in Florida, the Caribbean and Mexico.

An all wide-bodied fleet consists of one Boeing 747-200 and one ex-Delta Airbus Industrie A310-300 - both of which have been leased.

The livery adopted by Air Club International is illustrated by Airbus Industrie A310-324 C-GCIT. A white cabin exterior is interrupted only by the company name, which uses two different colour shades and three type styles/sizes. The word 'Air' is reproduced in solid blue upper case lettering, 'Club' is in green script and 'International' appears in a reduced upper case form. The focal point of the design is unquestionably the tail motif, where a large 'C' initial in flowing white script is reproduced over a blue painted backdrop.

AIR COLUMBUS

Air Columbus was formed in association with Sterling Airways and commenced operations on October 1st 1989 using a Boeing 727-200 leased from the Danish carrier. Based at Funchal (Madeira), the airline offers holiday charter flights from points in northern and western Europe.

Air Columbus has replaced Boeing 727 and 757 equipment leased from Sterling Airways with its own (leased) fleet of five 737-300s. However, it is possible that Boeing 757s will again be added at some point in the future.

The carrier's livery, illustrated by Boeing 737-33A CS-TKD, is based on a series of diagonal fuselage bands, which start at the nose as a midnight-blue coloured extension and become progressively 'thinner' in a rich, golden shade of yellow. Air Columbus titles are displayed in black upper case lettering on the cabin roof and overlap the fuselage bands, which peter out over the wing assembly. The entire concept is repeated on the fin, but with titles re-arranged in two lines to improve their visibility.

AIR CHARTER
F-GLGE

AIR CHINA
B-2458

C-GCIT
AIR Club
INTERNATIONAL

AIR COLUMBUS
CS-TKD
AIR COLUMBUS
TKD

AIR EUROPA

Air Europa (the operating title of Air Espana) was created in June 1986 by two Spanish financial institutions, Servicos Exteriores a Empresas SA and Soc. Bancayo de Promocion Empresa SA, in association with the now defunct International Leisure Group/Air Europe. Inclusive tour charters commenced in November of that year and are flown from points in northern and western Europe to holiday resorts in the Balearic and Canary Islands. Additional long haul destinations include Bangkok, Cairo, Cancun, Delhi, Halifax, Havana, Istanbul, New York, Santo Domingo and Salvador de Bahia.

A modern all-Boeing fleet currently includes ten 737-300s, three 737-400s (leased during the summer of 1994) and four 757-200/ERs.

Air Europa continues to use the livery it inherited from Air Europe, illustrated by Boeing 757-236 EC-FEF, with stylised 'AE' initials heading a four-tone cheatline composed of red and orange bands, which flows along the fuselage and flares as it meets the fin. Air Europa titles, in black lowercase lettering, are displayed alongside the Spanish flag on the forward cabin roof and repeated adjacent to the fin's leading edge. The red and orange fuselage and fin colouring is complimented by a white exterior finish. It should be noted that a similar livery is used by Air Europe Italy, which operates Boeing 767-300/ERs on long haul charter flights from several points within Italy.

AIR FRANCE

The history of the French flag carrier dates back to August 30th 1933 when a company called SCELA purchased the assets of Compagnie Aeropostale. After the war, Societe National Air France was formed, on January 1st 1946, rapidly reconstructing its impressive pre-war network and adding service to the Americas. Today, Air France is one of the world's leading international carriers, offering a vast network of scheduled passenger and freight services to points throughout the world.

For short to medium haul routes, Air France is equipped with a large fleet of Boeing 737s (-200/300/500s) and Airbus Industrie A320-100/200s, which are supplemented by A300B4s and A310-200/300s where additional capacity or range is required. Boeing 767-300/ERs provide service to Boston, Chicago, Miami, New York, San Francisco and Toronto, whilst Airbus A340-200/300s are used to other points in North and South America. For high capacity long haul passenger and cargo services Air France is also equipped with over fifty Boeing 747s (all models) and has additional aircraft on order. Completing the fleet composition and adding a touch of prestige, six Concorde 101s are on hand to fly daily (in each direction) between Paris and New York.

Air France was one of the first major airlines to discard cheatlines in favour of white overall fuselage colouring and when first introduced in 1975 its new image was both modern and innovative, setting standards for a new era in livery design. The livery illustrated by Concorde 101 F-BVFF is displayed by all members of the fleet, plus various commuter types operated on the company's behalf by an assortment of French regional airlines. The airline has, in recent times, experimented with a variety of metallic grey cheatline applications in an attempt to freshen up the design, but appears to have settled simply for a new corporate typeface.

AIR HONG KONG

Air Hong Kong was formed in November 1986 and commenced operations as a cargo charter carrier on February 4th 1988, initially with Boeing 707 equipment. Scheduled services were introduced on October 18th 1989 and now link Hong Kong with points in the Asia/Pacific region, the Middle East and Europe.

Two Boeing 747-100Fs and one 747-200F (all leased from Polaris) now equip the fleet, with additional capacity leased in as required.

Air Hong Kong's livery, illustrated by Boeing 747-132F VR-HKN, is one of the most colourful in today's vibrant air cargo industry. The fuselage, painted white to wing level and grey thereafter, features the corporate motif of red, orange and yellow 'AHK' initials, shaped in the form of an exotic bird. The yellow tail feathers extend to the lower forward fuselage before curling upwards into a red windowline, which leads from the nose in a conventional 'straight through' manner. Equal values of red, yellow and orange are used to colour the tail, with the upper bands guided by white contours originating from its leading edge. Air Hong Kong titles appear in black upper case lettering on the cabin roof, with their Cantonese equivalent displayed on the starboard side only.

AIR INDIA

Air India was established in March 1948 and became the country's designated international flag carrier following the nationalisation of air transport on August 1st 1953, when it also became a wholly state-owned corporation. The modern day Air India provides scheduled international services from Bombay, Delhi, Calcutta, Trivandrum and Madras to cities in Africa, Australia, Europe, the Middle and Far East, and North America, using a modern all-jet fleet.

Two main categories of aircraft are employed by Air India, one for regional services to the Middle and Far East and the other for high-density long-haul flights to Europe and beyond. The first category is currently filled by the Airbus Industrie A300B4 and A310-300, of which three and eight respectively are employed. For services to Australia, Africa, Europe and North America various members of the Boeing 747 family are used, including nine -200s, two -300s and four -400s. Future plans call for the regional fleet to be standardised on the A310-300 and for eight 747-400s to be in operation by 1996.

The livery illustrated by Boeing 747-437 VT-ESM was introduced by Air India in April 1971 and in earlier forms has been around considerably longer. In October 1989 Air India unveiled a brand new image, designed by Walter Landor Associates of San Francisco, which was intended to take the airline into the 'nineties. However, following a change of administration the new management took the unusual step of reverting to the carrier's previous 'Flying Palace' image, which is being re-introduced fleetwide.

air europa
air europa
EC-FEF
757

F-BVFF
AIR FRANCE

AIR HONG KONG

AIR-INDIA

AIR INTER

Air Inter was formed in 1954 and commenced operations four years later, in March 1958, over a network linking the cities of Paris, Strasbourg, Lyons, Nice, Marseille, Toulouse, Lordes/Tarbes, Bordeaux and Nantes. Today, the company maintains a thirty-seven point domestic network with a main hub at Paris, and also flies internationally to Dublin, Malaga, Palma de Mallorca, Porto, Seville, Shannon and Valencia.

A large fleet of Airbus A300B2/B4s, supplemented by the first of fifteen new A330-300s from January 1994, is operated on high density domestic flights such as Paris to Ajaccio, Bastia, Biarritz, Bordeaux, Brest, Lourdes, Marseille, Montpellier, Mulhouse, Nice, Nimes, Pau, Perpignan, Strasbourg, Toulon and Toulouse, as well as internationally to Malaga, Palma de Mallorca and Seville. Mainstay of the fleet is now the Airbus A320-200, of which thirty-five are in domestic and international use. In addition, seven 210-seat A321s are to be introduced from the summer of 1994 and nine 142-seat A319s have been ordered for delivery between July 1996 and mid-1997. It is likely that Air Inter will dispose of its A300B2/B4s as A330 deliveries progress and that any remaining Dassault Mercures will have no place in the carrier's all new Airbus fleet.

Air Inter's livery, illustrated by Airbus A320-211 F-GHQA, utilises the national colours of red, white and blue and is unquestionably brought to life by the lowering of a pale blue tint from the tail motif, bringing subtle colouring to the rear fuselage and lower fin areas. The design is balanced by 'Air Inter' titles, which appear in blue and red respectively alongside a scaled down motif.

AIR LANKA

Air Lanka was formed on January 10th 1979 to succeed Air Ceylon and today provides scheduled international services connecting the capital, Colombo, with cities throughout Asia, Europe and the Middle East.

Six Lockheed TriStars are used on services throughout the region and also serve Amsterdam, Frankfurt, London, Paris, Rome, Vienna and Zurich in Europe. Two Airbus Industrie A320-200s have replaced Boeing 737s in regional use, connecting Colombo with Abu Dhabi, Bangkok, Bombay, Delhi, Dubai, Karachi, Madras, Male, Tiruchirapaly and Tridandrum (supplementing TriStars on some routes). Three Airbus Industrie A340-300s have been ordered for delivery from September 1994.

Air Lanka continues to make use of the livery introduced by its initial fleet of Boeing 707s and 737s. The design centres on a bright red cheatline arrangement, which extends from the nose and eventually widens to colour the rear fuselage and fin, where it forms a solid backdrop for the company's stylised peacock motif. The whole fuselage is painted white overall with black 'Air Lanka' titles, alongside a representation of the Sri Lankan flag, displayed on the forward cabin roof.

AIR LIBERTE

Air Liberte was formed in July 1987 and commenced flying the following year, operating charters to European and Mediterranean holiday resorts in association with Club Aquarius. Long haul charters, to points in French Oceania and the Caribbean, were added during the summer of 1990, followed by a twice-weekly scheduled service connecting Paris with Montreal. (see also Air Liberte Tunisie)

The carrier's fleet currently includes eight McDonnell Douglas MD-83s (including two leased to Air Liberte Tunisie), one Airbus Industrie A310-300, two A300-600Rs and two McDonnell Douglas DC-10-30s.

Air Liberte's livery is based on the national colours of blue, white and red and features a curvaceous cheatline as its centrepiece. Bands of blue and red sweep up from the lower forward fuselage and peter out at windowlevel, re-emerging further along the cabin in yet another upward sweep. The curvature of the fuselage bands is emphasised in a more compact reproduction on the fin, which also accommodates a repetition of Air Liberte titles. The latter are displayed in blue lower case lettering, complete with red accents, and appear slightly offset. The patriotic image is complimented by a white painted cabin exterior, with the European Community flag applied to the engine housings.

AIR LIBERTE TUNISIE

Air Liberte Tunisie was formed in association with Air Liberte of France and commenced operations on October 5th 1990. Holiday charters are flown from points in Europe to the popular Tunisian resorts of Djerba, Monastir and Sfax.

The carrier is currently equipped with three McDonnell Douglas MD-83s, two of which are leased from Air Liberte and the other from the GPA Group.

McDonnell Douglas MD-83 F-GHEC illustrates the standard livery of Air Liberte Tunisie, which is based on the design of its French associate but reproduced in the Tunisian flag colours of red and white. Titles are displayed in French and Arabic and transposed to give each language precedence, with a different interpretation always appearing on the fin. The airline's nationality is confirmed by a small Tunisian flag which can be viewed on the engine housings.

QA
F-GHQA
AIR INTER
QA

TRISTAR
4R-ULJ
AIRLANKA

airLiberté
airLiberté
airLiberté

airLiberté
F-GHEC

AIR MALTA

The tiny Mediterranean island of Malta established its own international airline on April 1st 1973, with operations commencing later that year using Hawker Siddeley Tridents chartered from British Airways. Independent operations commenced one year later with the introduction of leased Boeing 720s and now connect Malta with thirty-one cities in Europe and seven in North Africa and the Middle East, all on a scheduled basis. Long haul services to Australia are planned for 1996.

Air Malta currently equipped with six Boeing 737-200s, three 737-300s and two Airbus Industrie A320-200s. An A310-300 has been leased from Lufthansa to provide additional capacity for the summer '94 season, and will no doubt lead to the introduction of Air Malta's own widebodied equipment in due course. Four 82-seat Avro International 146-RJ70ERs have been ordered for delivery between September 1994 and March 1995, to replace 737-200s.

The livery illustrated by Airbus Industrie A310-203 D-AICM is displayed by all current fleet members. The Cross of St. John, bestowed on the island in the middle ages, is an important feature of the design and appears in white within a red enclosure on the tail. Three solid blue stripes, representing the islands of Malta, Gozo and Comino, underscore the tail motif and then continue along the lower fuselage, with the cabin roof playing host to red 'Air Malta' titles.

AIR MAURITIUS

Air Mauritius was formed on June 14th 1967 as a multi-national venture between the Mauritian Government, Rogers & Co., Air France and BOAC, later joined by Air India. Operations commenced in August 1972 with a single Piper Navajo, flying to Rodrigues Island, but have since been expanded considerably. As well as commuter flights linking the capital, Port Louis, with neighbouring islands, scheduled international services are operated to Durban, Harare, Johannesburg and Nairobi within Africa, and further afield to Bombay, Frankfurt, Geneva, Hong Kong, Kuala Lumpur, London, Melbourne, Munich, Paris, Perth, Rome, Singapore and Zurich.

For local island hopping operations Air Mauritius is equipped with two ATR42s. Long haul capacity is provided by one Airbus Industrie A340-300 (leased from ILFC), two Boeing 767-200/ERs and three Boeing 747SPs. The airline has contracted to lease a second A340-300 from ILFC for introduction in late 1994.

The livery illustrated by Airbus Industrie A340-312 3B-NAT is worn by all types operated. The fuselage, all white down to wing level, sports an attractive bright red windowline trimmed below with a similarly coloured pinstripe, and bold upper case red 'Air Mauritius' titling alongside the national flag. The tail colouring compliments the cheatline in forming a backdrop for the company's motif, a red Falcon, which appears within a white enclosure.

AIR NAMIBIA

Air Namibia was originally formed as Namib Air in 1947 and adopted its present title on October 15th 1991. The airline's scheduled network now reaches as far as London, which is served three times weekly using leased Boeing 747SP equipment. In addition, Air Namibia also serves local communities from the capital, Windhoek, as well as providing service to Johannesburg, Harare, Capetown and Lusaka in Africa.

A fleet of three 19-seat Beech 1900Cs operate locally to Keetmanshoop, Luderitz, Maun, Mokuti Lodge, Mpacha, Ondangwa, Oranjemund, Rundu, Swakopmund, Rundu, Swakopmund, Tsumeb and Victoria Falls, as well as flying additional off-peak services to Johannesburg and Cape Town. A single Boeing 737-200 is used on regional trunk routes to South Africa, Zimbabwe and Zambia, with two Boeing 747SPs (leased from South African Airways) providing long haul service to Frankfurt and London. Between trips to Europe, the 747SPs are also used to provide additional capacity between Windhoek and Johannesburg, a route which is served by all types operated.

Air Namibia has extracted two colours from the national flag of blue, yellow, red and green to create a livery that is perhaps typically African in its design. Illustrated by Boeing 747SP-44 V5-SPF, the livery takes its inspiration from the sun and is therefore predominantly yellow with secondary blue colouring. The combination has been used to good effect, especially in the design of the tail motif where a flying crane appears in silhouette form against a bright yellow sun.

AIR NEW ZEALAND

The national airline of New Zealand was formed on April 1st 1978 as the result of a merger between New Zealand National Airways Corp. and Air New Zealand, which had been responsible for domestic and international operations respectively. Today, the carrier flies internationally to Adelaide, Apia (Samoa), Bangkok, Brisbane, Cairns, Denpasar-Bali, Hong Kong, Honolulu, Los Angeles, Melbourne, Nadi (Fiji), Nagoya, Noumea, Papeete, Perth, Rarotonga, Seoul, Singapore, Sydney, Taipei, Tokyo and Tongatapu (Tonga), as well as Frankfurt and London in Europe. Domestic services link Auckland, Christchurch, Dunedin, Invercargill, Norfolk Island, Palmerston, Queenstown and Wellington.

A fleet of twelve Boeing 737-200s is kept busy on domestic schedules, with seven 767-200/ERs, seven 767-300/ERs and five 747-200s used mostly within the Far East and Pacific region. Four 747-400s are used on flights to Frankfurt, Honolulu, London, Los Angeles, Melbourne and Sydney.

The design illustrated by Boeing 747-419 ZK-NBS was introduced by the original Air New Zealand in 1973, five years prior to the merger with NZNAC. Twin 'straight-through' cheat-lines in deep blue and turquoise underline blue Air New Zealand roof titling, which appears in a unique typeface alongside the national flag. This elegant colour combination, evoking images of the Pacific, is repeated on the fin and provides the setting for a traditional Maori symbol, known as the Koru.

AIR MALTA
D-AICM

AIR MAURITIUS

Air Namibia

air new zealand

AIR SEYCHELLES

Air Seychelles is the government-owned airline of the Seychelles which, until November 1985, confined its activities to inter-island flying. Today, the airline provides scheduled international connections from Mahe Island to cities in Africa, the Middle and Far East and Europe, as well as regular, high frequency services to the Praslin Islands.

For scheduled and charter activities around the islands Air Seychelles employs a busy fleet of four DHC-6 Twin Otters and one Britten-Norman Islander. Up to eighteen daily roundtrips are scheduled to and from the Praslin Islands, mostly early morning and late afternoon, with each one way trip having a duration of fifteen minutes. Internationally, Air Seychelles uses a Boeing 757 on routes to Bahrain, Dubai, Johannesburg, Madrid, Nairobi and Singapore, whilst a higher capacity Boeing 767-200/ER serves Frankfurt, London, Paris, Rome and Zurich. Both aircraft are leased from ILFC.

The livery illustrated by Boeing 767-2Q8/ER S7-AAS was introduced by Air Seychelles in 1985 and takes its red and green colouring from the national flag. The tail motif, which features a pair of fairy terns, signifies paradise in the form of love and harmony. The livery is concluded with blue 'Air Seychelles' titling, appearing on the cabin roof alongside the national flag.

AIRTOURS INTERNATIONAL

Manchester-based Airtours International was formed in 1990 and commenced operations in March 1991 with three newly delivered McDonnell Douglas MD-83s. The airline currently provides inclusive-tour services to holiday resorts in Europe and the Mediterranean, the Caribbean, Africa, Mexico and the United States, with programmes to Sydney (Australia) and Las Vegas due to begin during the winter 1994/95 season. Flights originate from several UK departure points, including Birmingham, Cardiff, East Midlands, Glasgow, Liverpool, London-Gatwick/Stansted, Manchester and Newcastle. The company acquired Cardiff-based Inter European Airways on October 31st 1993 and purchased SAS Leisure's interest in the Scandinavian charter airline Premiair in early 1994.

The airline continues to use two Airbus Industrie A320-200s and two Boeing 757s inherited from Inter European Airways, alongside its existing fleet of eight McDonnell Douglas MD-83s (leased from the GPA Group) and two Boeing 767-300/ERs. However, it is likely that more A320-200s (up to twelve) will be acquired to replace the MD-83s and Boeing 757s in the interests of fleet standardisation.

A bold visual image, illustrated by McDonnell Douglas MD-83 G-TTPT, promotes high visibility Airtours titling over the lower forward fuselage, which is white down to wing level and dark blue thereafter. A turquoise coloured pinstripe lines the underside and rides up the fin's leading edge, regenerating at the rear to form two additional lines of unequal length. The tail colouring is not unlike Garuda's and features an encircled letter 'A' motif in contrasting shades of blue and turquoise.

AIR TRANSAT

Air Transat was created in December 1986 and is now Canada's largest international and domestic charter carrier, serving holiday destinations in Mexico, the Caribbean, Belgium, France, Germany, Greece, Holland, Ireland, Italy, Poland, Portugal, Ukraine, the United Kingdom and the USA, principally from Montreal and Toronto.

The carrier is currently equipped with a fleet of three Boeing 727-200s, four Boeing 757-200s and five Lockheed TriStars.

The livery illustrated by Boeing 757-23A C-GTSF is now worn by all types operated. The fuselage, all white to wing level and natural metal thereafter, is coloured by a dark blue cheatline arrangement which leads from the nose in a conventional manner and then splits to form a bold windowline with underlying trim. The windowline eventually flares in an upward sweep over the fin, edged by a parallel band of red which bleeds from the lower line. Stylised 'AT' initials form a white tail motif, which is repeated on the cabin roof (within black Air Transat titles) and engine housings in red and blue respectively.

AIR UK

Air UK was created in January 1980 through the marriage of several smaller domestic and regional operators, including British Island Airways, Air Anglia, Air West and Air Wales. Today, Air UK serves Aberdeen, Edinburgh, Glasgow, Belfast, Newcastle, Teesside, Leeds/Bradford, Humberside, Norwich, London-Heathrow/Gatwick and Stansted, Southampton, Guernsey and Jersey domestically, with international connections offered to Bergen, Stavanger, Amsterdam, Brussels, Dusseldorf, Frankfurt, Paris, Nice, Innsbruck and Florence. The company's base and principle traffic hub is located at London-Stansted.

A large fleet is mostly standardised on Fokker equipment, with seventeen F-27 Friendships, eight Fokker 50 turboprops and nine 101-seat Fokker 100s operating at the heart of the airline's domestic and international network. Two 35-seat Shorts 360s continue to be used on 'thinner' routes, with ten British Aerospace 146s (including seven 110-seat -300s) providing additional capacity.

The livery illustrated by Fokker 100 G-UKFC was introduced in July 1992 but is yet to be applied fleetwide. Based on a previous design, now used by affiliate Air UK Leisure, the revised livery features a deep blue cheatline which rises from below window level to colour the rear fuselage and fin. A fluttering half union flag motif graphically emphasises the airline's nationality and is supported by a pale blue 'mast', which also forms part of the cheatline arrangement. Air UK titles complete the livery and are displayed in blue lettering on the forward cabin roof.

Air Seychelles
S7-AAX

G-TTPT
Airtours

air Transat
at
C-GTSF

AirUK
G-UKFC

AIR UK LEISURE

Air UK Leisure was created as a sister company of Air UK to serve the European leisure market, offering charter services from London-Gatwick/Stansted, Birmingham, Manchester and other UK airports to holiday destinations in Europe, the Mediterranean and Canary Islands. Operations commenced on April 30th 1988. Leisure International Airways is a wholly-owned subsidiary that was formed on February 18th 1992 to operate European and long haul charter routes from London-Gatwick and Manchester (in association with Unijet).

Air UK Leisure is currently equipped with a fleet of seven Boeing 737-400s (including three leased from the GPA Group), whereas its Leisure International Airways subsidiary employs two 767-300/ERs.

The livery used by Air UK Leisure (and Leisure International Airways) is based on a design that was first introduced by Air UK in 1987. Illustrated by Boeing 737-42C G-UKLC, it features cylinderical cheatlines of dark, medium and pale blue, which start at different points along the forward fuselage and merge upwards at the rear. Guided by a narrow red pinstripe, the darker cheatline forms a mast for the half union flag motif, which dominates a white painted fin. Blue Air UK titles are displayed in the carrier's standard corporate typeface, with the word 'Leisure' applied in a red freestyle script. Note: the Boeing 767-300/ERs of Leisure International Airways simply display 'Leisure' titles without any reference to Air UK.

AIR UKRAINE (AVIALINII UKRAINY)

Air Ukraine was formed in 1991 to supplant a major Aeroflot Directorate based in the capital, Kiev. Although domestic and regional operations remain much the same as before, scheduled international connections have been expanded and now link Kiev with Athens, Beijing, Cairo, Chicago, Damascus, New York, Prague (also from Lvov), Sharjah, Sofia, Tel Aviv, Tianjin, Warsaw (also from Lvov) and Washington, with many other worldwide destinations served on a charter basis. In addition, a separate joint venture airline known as Air Ukraine International was created in October 1992 to serve the western European cities of Amsterdam, Berlin, Brussels, Frankfurt, London, Manchester, Munich, Paris and Vienna, using two Boeing 737-400s leased from the GPA Group.

Domestic and regional capacity is provided by a large fleet of Antonov An-24/26s and Yakovlev Yak-40s, supplemented by a smaller number of An-30/An-32s and Let 410s. For short to medium operations Air Ukraine is equipped with several Tupolev Tu-134As, Tu-154s and Yakovlev Yak-42s, with seven Ilyushin Il-62Ms (including six acquired from LOT) serving on routes to China, Sharjah and North America. Two Ilyushin Il-18s have also been added to the fleet inherited from Aeroflot.

The carrier's livery is based on the Ukrainean flag colours of blue and yellow, of which various different shades have been used in repainting the fleet. In its complete form, illustrated by Ilyushin Il-62M UR-86134, the design is both modern and attractive and colours the entire rear fuselage and fin. Air Ukraine titles are accompanied by a Cyrillic interpretation on the forward fuselage, and also by the national flag, with the carrier's motif appearing within a yellow sphere on the fin. The livery adopted by Air Ukraine International shares many common features and is similarly balanced.

AIR ZIMBABWE

Air Zimbabwe was formed in September 1967 as Air Rhodesia, with the current name adopted when Rhodesia became Zimbabwe in April 1980. Scheduled passenger services link the capital, Harare, with other cities and tourist attractions in Zimbabwe, with international connections to Southern and East Africa and Europe. Australia is also served under a code-sharing agreement with Qantas.

For domestic and regional services Air Zimbabwe uses three Boeing 737-200s and one British Aerospace 146-200, supplemented by two Boeing 707-320Bs which have now been retired from long haul use. The larger Boeings are used mainly between Harare and Victoria Falls, which is a popular route with tourists, and on a weekly service to Mauritius. Two Boeing 767-200/ERs are used on services to Frankfurt, Johannesburg, Larnaca, London and Nairobi.

The current Air Zimbabwe livery, illustrated by Boeing 767-2N0/ER Z-WPF, was introduced in early 1984 to replace an earlier Air Rhodesia design. A quadruple cheatline in the national colours of green, yellow, red and black commences at the nose and steps up to the windowline, eventually colouring the lower half of the tail with a second upward sweep from the rear fuselage. A stylised yellow bird motif is embraced by the red star of socialism in the upper half of the fin, with simple lower case 'Air Zimbabwe' lettering displayed alongside a wavering portrayal of the national flag on the forward cabin roof.

AIR 2000

Air 2000 was formed in 1986 as a subsidiary of Owners Abroad and commenced operations in April 1987 using two leased Boeing 757s. Inclusive-tour charters are flown from Birmingham, Glasgow, London-Gatwick and Manchester to holiday destinations in Canada, the Caribbean, Europe, Gambia, Kenya, Mexico and the United States. The carrier also operates scheduled year-round services connecting Gatwick with Larnaca and Paphos.

Today, Air 2000 is equipped with a fleet of fourteen Boeing 757-200s, of which four are normally operated by its Canada 3000 affiliate during the winter months, and four smaller Airbus Industrie A320-200s.

The livery illustrated by Boeing 757-28A G-OOOD has been adopted by Air 2000 and Canada 3000 Airlines to facilitate the seasonal interchange of aircraft between the two carriers. A white cabin exterior promotes twin narrow cheatlines of red and gold, which flare as they sweep onto the base of the tail. Similarly coloured Air 2000 titling is displayed on the forward section of the cabin roof and more prominently on the fin, with the red and gold theme also used to colour the engine housings in a move which unquestionably adds the perfect finishing touch.

AirUK Leisure
G-UKLC
Flagship St Christopher

AIR UKRAINE
АВІАЛІНІЇ УКРАЇНИ
UR-86134

air zimbabwe
Z-WPF
BOEING 767-200 ER

AIR 2000
AIR 2000
G-OOOO

ALITALIA

The Italian national flag carrier was formed in September 1946 under the name of Aerolinee Italiene Internazionali (Alitalia), in association with BEA, to operate converted war surplus bombers over a domestic passenger network. In 1948, the first international flights, to Buenos Aires, took place and the present title was adopted in October 1957 when the company was merged with Linee Aeree Italiene. An extensive route system of passenger and freight services now connects Italy with major cities in all five continents. Domestically, Alitalia maintains a comprehensive network to compliment that of its Naples-based subsidiary, ATI.

McDonnell Douglas DC-9-30s and MD-80s currently form the nucleus of the fleet, with fourteen Airbus A300B4s providing additional capacity on major domestic and European trunk routes. However, the airline has ordered a total of forty Airbus Industrie A321-100s to replace DC-9-30s from the summer of 1994. For long haul operations Alitalia is equipped with eight McDonnell Douglas MD-11Cs and thirteen Boeing 747-200s (including two freighters).

The image, designed by Walter Landor Associates to take Alitalia into the seventies and illustrated by Airbus A321-112 I-BIXA, was widely regarded as the most modern and stylish of its time. The livery's centrepiece is an ingenious 'A' logo in green with a red centre, which is formed on the tail as a continuation of the simple green windowline and repeated within the black 'Alitalia' fuselage lettering, in black and red. A small but distinguishing feature is the placing of white 'Alitalia' titles within the cheatline arrangement, adjacent to each passenger entrance.

ALL NIPPON AIRWAYS-ANA

All Nippon Airways was formed in 1958 through the merger of Far Eastern Airlines and Japan Helicopter and Aeroplane Transport Co. and over the years has grown to become Japan's largest passenger airline. International services were launched in March 1986 and now connect Tokyo with several major cities throughout the Asia/Pacific region, plus Frankfurt, London, Los Angeles, New York, Paris and Washington. An vast domestic network is also maintained by All Nippon Airways and its Air Nippon subsidiary.

The domestic and regional passenger market in Japan is so immense that All Nippon is able to employ sixteen purpose built Boeing 747-100SRs, nine 747-400Ds, twenty-five 767-200s, thirty-three 767-300s and five Lockheed TriStars on relatively short haul sectors, supplemented by twelve Airbus Industrie A320-200 narrowbodies. NAMC YS-11s, Boeing 737-200s and four additional A320s have been transferred to its Air Nippon subsidiary. Long haul capacity is currently provided by six 747-200s, nine 747-400s and four 767-300/ERs. Fifteen 777-200s, five A340-300s, four A320-200s and eight 747-400s are on order.

The livery illustrated by Boeing 747-481 JA8958 was introduced in April 1983 to coincide with the delivery of the company's first Boeing 767. An angular cheatline arrangement, in shades of dark and medium blue, starts level with a grey painted underside and flares to colour the upper rear fuselage and fin. 'ANA' initials form the tail motif and are also reproduced on the cabin roof in Japanese, appearing between black All Nippon Airways titling and the national flag. Note: one Boeing 747-400D and one 767-300 have been painted in special multi-coloured liveries based on marine life and are affectionately known as 'Marine Jumbo' and 'Marine Jumbo Junior'.

ALYEMDA

Alyemda was formed by presidential decree on March 11th 1961 as the national airline of the People's Democratic Republic of the Yemen, formerly known as Aden or South Yemen. Today, the carrier offers scheduled international services to Abu Dhabi, Amman, Bombay, Cairo, Damascus, Djibouti, Doha, Dubai, Jeddah, London and Sharjah. In addition, local services connect Aden with Al Ghaydah, Ataq and Riyan/Mukalla, as well as Sanaa in the north.

Domestic and regional flights are generally operated by two Boeing 737-200s, with a larger 707-320C providing additional capacity on services linking Aden and Riyan/Mukalla with Jeddah. A single Dash 7 (another is stored) flies domestically between Aden and Seiyun. For its routes to Bombay, Dubai, London and Sharjah, Alyemda is equipped with a widebodied Airbus Industrie A310-300.

Airbus Industrie designed a new livery to mark the delivery of A310-304 F-ODSV (illustrated) to Alyemda in May 1993. Based on a white cabin exterior, the design centres on a blue, black and red pinstriped cheatline - originating from black Alyemda lettering on the forward fuselage. Secondary Yemen Airlines titling is displayed above the airline's name in red, and repeated in Arabic along the upper rear fuselage. The tail motif has been reproduced within a metallic grey sphere, which is outlined in red and set against a solid blue backdrop, the latter also used to colour the engine housings of the A310.

AMBASSADOR AIRWAYS

Newcastle based Ambassador Airways was created in 1992 as a subsidiary of Best Leisure Travel Ltd and commenced operations the following summer with two Boeing 757s. The airline operates inclusive tour charters to holiday resorts in Europe and the Mediterranean region from a number of UK departure points, including London-Gatwick, Manchester and Newcastle.

A rapidly expanding fleet now includes four Boeing 757-200s, two Boeing 737-200s and two Airbus Industrie A320-200s, the latter operated on Ambassador's behalf by South East European Airlines of Greece. Most aircraft are operated on a seasonal basis and during the winter months excess capacity is leased out to other carriers.

In its complete form, illustrated by Boeing 757-236 G-BUDZ, the livery of Ambassador Airways features a combination of yellow, pale blue, red and yellow pinstripes over a medium blue coloured base, the latter also covering the fin. A yellow tail motif is composed of a series of double 'A' initials, which radiate from the centre of a circular enclosure below horizontal bands of yellow, red and pale blue. Ambassador titles are displayed in black upper case lettering on a white cabin roof, with the fuselage colours repeated on the engine housings. Note: the Boeing 737-200s wear a similar livery but with the fuselage pinstriping replaced by a more substantial band of yellow, whilst the A320s simply wear a white over finish with only black titles and the yellow tail motif applied.

Alitalia
I-BIXA

ANA
全日空
All Nippon Airways
JA8095

YEMEN AIRLINES
ALYEMDA
F-ODSV

AMBASSADOR

AMERICAN AIRLINES

This vast Texas-based carrier was formed in May 1934 as the successor to American Airways, itself formed in January 1930 through the merger of several smaller companies. In addition to extensive domestic operations, fed by the equally impressive 'American Eagle' commuter network, the carrier also flies internationally to Canada, Japan, Mexico, the Caribbean and to several major cities in Europe.

A major fleet renewal programme is currently in progress which will see types such as the Boeing 727-200 and McDonnell Douglas DC-10-10/30 disappear from American Airlines service in due course. The mainstay of domestic operations is now the McDonnell Douglas MD-80, of which some two hundred and sixty have been delivered to date. These are supplemented by a large fleet of Fokker 100s, Boeing 757s and 767s, with over one hundred 727-200s still to be phased out. Additional capacity is provided by thirty-five Airbus Industrie A300B4-600s, which in addition to mainland operations also feed the carrier's hub at San Juan (Puerto Rico). Long haul capability is provided by twenty McDonnell Douglas MD-11s and the Boeing 767 fleet, which includes ten 767-200s, twenty 767-200/ERs and over forty 767-300/ERs to meet both domestic and international requirements.

The present livery, illustrated by Airbus Industrie A300B4-605R N7082A, has stood the test of time extremely well despite the fact that modern manufacturing techniques now restrict the traditional bare metal appearance, which has become something of a company trademark. Introduced in 1969, the livery features triple cheatlines of blue, white and red, complimented by red 'American' titles which are outlined in white. The tail hosts the company motif of a blue eagle swooping down between the peaks of double 'A' initials.

AMERICAN TRANS AIR

Indianapolis based American Trans Air was certificated by the Federal Aviation Administration in March 1981 as a supplemental air carrier, after its formation by Captain George Mikelsons. Scheduled passenger services are currently provided from Indianapolis and Chicago to Ft. Lauderdale, Ft. Myers, Las Vegas, Orlando, Sarasota and St. Petersburg. Cancun, Nassau, Montego Bay, St. Thomas and St. Croix are also served from Indianapolis, with connections to Miami, Phoenix and West Palm Beach offered from Chicago only. American Trans Air is also the U.S. flag carrier to Nigeria with a twice-weekly service between New York and Lagos (via Santa Maria). Other scheduled routes connect New York and Detroit with Belfast and Riga (Latvia), and San Francisco with Honolulu and Kahului. In addition, charter services are flown throughout the world.

For domestic and regional operations American Trans Air employs a fleet of sixteen Boeing 727-200s and six 757-200s. Long haul capacity is provided by twelve Lockheed TriStars, which operate the scheduled flights to Hawaii and Nigeria as well as charters to Europe etc. The Boeing 757s are also used on scheduled and non-scheduled transatlantic flights.

An extremely stylish colourscheme, illustrated by Lockheed TriStar-50 N188AT, features a triple 'straight-through' cheatline in gold, white and blue, above and below which the fuselage is painted white and grey respectively. A cleverly designed tail motif illustrates a symbolic runway approach using the company's 'ATA' initials in gold and blue, and is repeated alongside the fuselage titles.

AOM FRENCH AIRLINES

AOM French Airlines was created in 1987 as Air Outre Mer and adopted its present title following a merger with Minerve in 1992. From its base at Paris Orly the company provides scheduled long haul services to Bangkok, Cayenne (French Guiana), Fort de France (Martinique), Havana, Ho Chi Minh City, Jeddah, Karachi, Los Angeles, Moscow, Papeete (Tahiti), Pointe-a-Pitre (Guadeloupe), St. Denis (Reunion Island), St. Martin (Netherlands Antilles) and Tokyo-Narita. Domestically, regular daily services are flown between Paris and Nice, although Marseille and Mulhouse also serve as pick up points on some of the long haul flights to French territories in the Pacific and Caribbean. The charter activities of Minerve have also been absorbed by the company.

The requirements of AOM French Airlines are met by two types of aircraft, the high capacity McDonnell Douglas DC-10-30 for scheduled long-haul and high density charter operations, and the narrow bodied MD-83 to cover domestic flights and thinner charter routes to the Mediterranean.

The livery adopted by the company is simple but effective and basically follows the design parameters established by Air Outre Mer. A white overall fuselage and fin plays host to blue 'AOM' initials, the top of which have been outlined in red to complete the French tri-colour. Minerve's contribution to the livery is a secondary motif, which can be found beneath the cockpit windows of the McDonnell Douglas DC-10-30 illustrated. The only notable variation is the application of 'Cubana' titles for one of the twice-weekly services to Havana, which is flown on the Cuban airline's behalf.

ARIANA AFGHAN AIRLINES

In recent times the flying activities of Ariana have been hampered by internal unrest and fuel shortages, but since the Soviet withdrawal the airline has re-equipped with former Air France Boeing 727-200s and resumed service to international points such as London and Paris. Domestic flights appear to be operated on a fuel available basis and tickets for such must be purchased locally and at the time of travel.

Domestic services (all subject to confirmation) link the capital, Kabul, with Bamiyan, Bost, Chakcharan, Faizabad, Farah, Gardez, Herat, Jalalabad, Kandahar, Khost, Khwahan, Kunduz, Maimana, Mazar-I-Sharif, Qala-Nau, Sheghnan, Tirinkot and Zaranj, and are flown with Antonov An-24, An-26, Yakovlev Yak-40, DHC-6 Twin Otter and Boeing 727 equipment. Internationally, the airline uses two 727-100Cs and three 727-200s on services to Amritsar (India), Dubai, Istanbul, London, Moscow, Paris, Peshawar (Pakistan), Tashkent and Tehran. The Boeing 727-100Cs are operated in a combi configuration, carrying both passengers and freight, and serve regional markets as well as Kandahar and Mazar-I-Sharif domestically. Service to Delhi is provided by two Tupolev Tu-154Ms, which also supplement the '727s to routes to Moscow and Tashkent.

Air India is not the only airline to revive a former image as the livery illustrated by Boeing 727-228 YA-FAY was made redundant by Ariana in September 1979 and then re-adopted several years later, following a merger with Bakhtar Afghan Airlines and the subsequent renaming of the national carrier. The most distinguishing feature of the design is the aggressive looking bird of prey motif, which is believed to symbolise the undying spirit of the Afghan people.

American
AA

AMERICAN TRANS AIR
Britannia
AIR 2000

AOM
AOM
F-GGMZ

ARIANA
YA-FAY

ASA - AFRICAN SAFARI AIRWAYS

Basle/Mulhouse based African Safari Airways was created in August 1967 by the African Tourist Development Agency, in association with African Safari Lodges, to serve Kenya's thriving tourist industry - bringing holidaymakers to the game parks of East Africa from cities in Germany, Switzerland and the United Kingdom. All services are flown on an inclusive-tour charter basis and currently connect Mombassa with several points in Europe.

The airline is equipped with a single McDonnell Douglas DC-10-30 which it acquired from KLM in December 1992. A second aircraft may be added following the recent sale of two DC-8-60s, especially if newly proposed routes to London and Manchester are added to the carrier's charter network.

With the introduction of DC-10-30 PH-DTL (illustrated) the African Safari name was completely dropped from the livery and replaced by the initials 'ASA' in dark blue. At the same time a bold red cheatline disappeared and a series of red and blue pinstripes were placed below the window line, dissecting the white (upper) and grey (lower) fuselage colouring. Of the four pinstripes displayed, only two appear below the 'ASA' lettering and these are pale blue in colour. A Zebra-striped fin is underscored by a narrow red pinstripe, offering a clean and tidy edge above the raised engine - which is itself used to promote additional 'ASA' initials.

AUSTRIAN AIRLINES

The Austrian national carrier came into being on September 30th 1957, following an agreement to merge two projected companies, Air Austria and Austrian Airways. However, the company's first service did not take place until March 31st 1958 when a flight between Vienna and London was completed. Today, Austrian Airlines maintains a comprehensive network of scheduled services within Europe, also connecting Vienna with cities in North America and the Middle and Far East. Scheduled domestic services are the responsibility of a separate subsidiary, Austrian Air Services, which uses Fokker 50 equipment.

Austrian Airlines turned to the McDonnell Douglas MD-80 family when its long serving DC-9-30 fleet became due for renewal. The airline now operates twenty of these aircraft, made of up seven MD-81s, six MD-82s, two MD-83s and five MD-87s, on services within Europe and to the Middle East. Additional capacity is provided by four Airbus Industrie A310-300s which, in addition to supplementing the MD-80 on high density European routes, also provide service to Chicago, New York and Tokyo. Austrian Airlines will eventually standardise on Airbus Industrie equipment and has ordered seven A320s, six A321s and two A340-200s for future fleet introduction.

The simple but delicate livery, illustrated by Airbus Industrie A310-325 OE-LAD, has remained basically unchanged since the company's foundation. The red, white and red tail arrangement proudly underlines its national identity and is complimented by 'Austrian' titles and the familiar chevron motif, which appear in a matching shade of red on the forward cabin.

AVIACO

Aviaco was formed by a group of businessmen in the industrial town of Bilbao in 1948, initially to fly perishable goods with a small fleet of Bristol Freighters. Passenger operations followed with the introduction of regular services connecting Bilbao with Madrid and Barcelona in 1950. These routes were progressively expanded to supplement the domestic network of the national carrier - Iberia, which later went on to become Aviaco's principle shareholder in 1954. In April 1971 the role of Aviaco was extended to include IT charter operations and during the years that followed it became one of Europe's leading holiday charter airlines. Today, Aviaco functions mainly as scheduled domestic carrier, operating a large all-jet fleet on services throughout the Spanish mainland and to the Balearic and Canary Islands. A modest international network connects Asturias, Jerez De La Frontera and Zaragoza with London-Stansted, and Jerez De La Frontera with Paris-Orly.

A fleet standardised on members of the McDonnell Douglas DC-9/MD-80 family currently includes twenty-one DC-9-30s (mostly ex-Iberia) and thirteen MD-88s, of which Aviaco is the sole European operator.

The livery illustrated by McDonnell Douglas DC-9-32 EC-BYI is worn by all fleet members. Although less colourful than previous applications, the design reflects Aviaco's primary role as a scheduled domestic carrier and is therefore more businesslike in appearance. The cheatline arrangement uses three shades of blue, the darkest of which also colours the titles and tail motif. A stylised letter 'A' acts as the corporate symbol, fronting 'Aviaco' titles on the cabin roof and 'AYC' initials on the engine housings, whilst appearing by itself on the tail. The name Aviaco is an acronym of Aviacion y Comercio, from which the 'AYC' initials originate.

AZERBAIJAN AIRLINES/AHY

Azerbaijan Airlines, known locally as Azarbaycan Hava Yollari, was created in 1991 to assume the domestic and international operations of a regional Aeroflot Directorate. Services currently link the capital, Baku, with Ankara, Cologne, Dubai, Istanbul, London, Sharjah and Tehran. Routes inherited from Aeroflot include connections from Baku to Minsk (Belorussia), Alma Ata and Shevchenko (Kazakhstan); Krasnodar, Moscow, Sochi and St. Petersburg (Russian Federation); Kiev and Simferopol (Ukraine); and Nukus and Samarkland (Uzbekistan). From the second major city of Gyandzha, connections are provided to Baku; Mineralnye Vody, Moscow and St. Petersburg (Russian Federation); and Kiev (Ukraine). An extensive domestic network is also maintained.

For domestic and regional operations Azerbaijan Airlines is equipped with a small fleet of Antonov An-26s and An-32s, about a dozen Yakovlev Yak-40s and some Mil Mi-8 helicopters. Tupolev Tu-134s are also used on domestic trunk routes and supplement larger Tu-154s on international services. At least eleven Tu-134s and sixteen Tu-154s are known to serve with the carrier. The airline has acquired two Boeing 727-200s for use on services to Ankara, Cologne, Istanbul and London, and operates a leased Boeing 707-320C freighter in association with Buffalo Airways of the United States. Two Ilyushin Il-76MDs have also been acquired.

An attractive arrangement of green, blue, orange and blue colours a bold windowline, which is complimented by red 'Azerbaijan Airlines' titles and blue 'AHY' initials. Towards the rear of the fuselage the cheatline flares in an unusual manner, with the orange line forking to direct green and blue colouring onto the fin. The tail motif features a stylised bird alongside 'AZAL' initials, which both appear in blue within an orange sphere. The livery is known to be worn by Boeing 727-200s, Tu-134s, Tu-154s, Yak-40s and Mil Mi-8 helicopters.

ASA
ASA

AUSTRIAN
OE-LAD

EC-BYI
AVIACO

AZAL
AZERBAIJAN AIRLINES
4K-85274

BALKAN - BULGARIAN AIRLINES

Based in the capital, Sofia, the Bulgarian flag carrier connects this eastern European state with major cities in Africa, Asia, Europe and North America, as well as providing a comprehensive domestic route network. The company can trace its history back to June 29th 1947 and was operated from 1948 as a joint Bulgarian-Soviet venture under the name of TASBO, becoming wholly Bulgarian-owned by 1954.

Most scheduled international services are now flown with modern western-built equipment, which includes four Airbus Industrie A320-200s, three Boeing 737-500s and two 767-200/ERs - all of which are leased. These continue to be supplemented by a large fleet of Tupolev Tu-154s, although passenger operations with the less fuel efficient Russian jets are now mostly confined to inclusive tour charters feeding the Black Sea resorts of Bourgas and Varna. For domestic and regional operations Balkan is equipped with fourteen Antonov An-24Bs and a small fleet of Tupolev Tu-134As. Additional cargo capacity is provided by Antonov An-12s and a handful of converted Ilyushin Il-18s.

The livery illustrated by Boeing 767-27E/ER F-GHGD is worn by all fleet members. Based on the national colours of green and red, it starts out as a conventional cheatline arrangement but becomes more adventurous immediately beyond the wing assembly area, where it fans out and wraps around the underside of the fuselage. The sweep of the lines is reversed on the tail to create a bold national identity, which is also very modern in appearance. Bold red 'Balkan' titling appears on the cabin roof, in English on the starboard side and Bulgarian on the port, accompanied in both cases by green 'Bulgarian Airlines' sub-titles in English, as well as the traditional 'shooting star' motif in red.

BANGLADESH BIMAN

The national airline of Bangladesh was formed in January 1972, shortly after the country obtained its independence from Pakistan. Scheduled passenger services commenced in February of that year and now connect the capital Dhaka with points in Europe, the Middle East and Asia, as well as linking several domestic cities.

Bangladesh Biman uses five McDonnell Douglas DC-10-30s on services to Abu Dhabi, Amsterdam, Athens, Bangkok, Bombay, Delhi, Doha, Dubai, Frankfurt, Hong Kong, Jeddah, Karachi, Kuala Lumpur, Kuwait, London, Muscat, New York, Paris, Riyadh, Singapore and Tokyo. For domestic operations, the carrier is equipped with two British Aerospace ATPs and two Fokker F.28-4000 Fellowships, the latter also used on 'thinner' regional routes to Calcutta and Kathmandu. The airline is also planning to add two Airbus A310-300s.

The current Bangladesh Biman livery, illustrated by McDonnell Douglas DC-10-30 S2-ACP, uses the flag colours of red and green to colour a simple straight-through cheatline arrangement and twin horizontal fin bands. Black titles are carried alongside the national flag in English and Bengali on the port and starboard sides respectively, reading as 'Bangladesh Airlines' on the forward cabin roof and 'Biman' on the tail. The motif, which represents a white stork flying across a setting sun, is displayed centrally on the fin.

BELAVIA

Belavia was created in 1992 to provide services from the Belorussian capital, Minsk, in place of the former Aeroflot Directorate previously serving the region. Scheduled passenger services are currently flown to Berlin, Frankfurt, Shannon, Vienna and Zurich, as well as Kiev (Ukraine), Tashkent (Uzbekistan) and Ekaterinburg, Krasnodar, Mineralnye Vody, Moscow, Murmansk, Nizhnvartovsk, Nizhniy Novgorod, Samara, Sochi and Voronezh (Russian Federation). Service is also provided within the Belorussian Republic.

The fleet inherited from Aeroflot includes twelve Antonov An-24s, seven An-26s, twenty-three Tu-134As, fourteen Tu-154s and four Yakovlev Yak-40s, with additional cargo capacity reportedly provided by two Ilyushin Il-76s.

In its original form, the livery illustrated by Tupolev Tu-134A EW-65754 featured red 'Byelorus' titles with the Belorussian flag displayed on the tail. The name 'Belavia' and the motif that now adorns the fin came later, but has since been applied to most members of the fleet. The flag, which initially covered most of the fin, now sits behind the motif in a scaled down form. The former cheatline arrangement of Aeroflot remains, presumably as a cost saving measure, but blends well with the blue coloured tail and engine housings.

BRAATHENS SAFE

Formed by the Braathens Shipping company in March 1946, Braathens SAFE is today Norway's premier domestic and charter airline, offering scheduled passenger services which link major Norwegian towns and cities; including Oslo, Kristiansand, Kristiansund, Stavanger, Bergen, Aalesund, Molde, Roros, Trondheim, Bodo, Evenes and Tromso. Scheduled international services connect Oslo with Alicante, Billund, London, Malaga, Malmo and Newcastle, whilst inclusive tour charters are flown to holiday destinations throughout Europe and North Africa.

A modern all-jet fleet is almost exclusively equipped with CFM-powered members of the Boeing 737 family. Although some earlier 737-200s still remain, the majority are leased out to other carriers and will eventually give way to the newer 737-400 and -500 models, of which seven and twenty-one respectively have been delivered to date.

The livery illustrated by Boeing 737-505 LN-BRC was introduced in April 1984 to coincide with the introduction of the company's first Boeing 767-200, a type which has since left the fleet. The basic design was nothing new, with the most significant change being the lowering of cheatlines to a new location beneath the windowline. The tail plays host to the Norwegian flag, from which the blue and red colouring originates, and deep blue 'Braathens S.A.F.E' titling occupies much of the cabin roof. Note that 'S.A.F.E' stands for South American and Far East Air Transport as a reminder of the company's formative years, but has been retained in view of its obvious marketing appeal.

БАЛКАН
BULGARIAN AIRLINES
F-GHGD
767-200ER

BELAVIA
EW-65754
TU-134A

BRAATHENS S·A·F·E
LN-BRC
BRC

BRITANNIA AIRWAYS

Britain's premier charter airline, Britannia Airways flies inclusive tour charters from cities throughout the United Kingdom to over 100 worldwide destinations, with blanket coverage of Mediterranean holiday resorts in Europe and North Africa. The company was formed in December 1961 as Euravia (London) Ltd., with the present title being adopted in August 1964 and a take over by the Thomson Organisation taking place the following year. The airline is based at Luton Airport, but also flies extensively from London (Gatwick), Manchester and many other UK Airports.

Britannia Airways retired its last Boeing 737-200 in March 1994 and its fleet is now standardised on Boeing 757 and 767-200 equipment. These aircraft provide greater range and capacity and have enabled tour operators such as Thomson Holidays to develop new 'far away' holiday packages to points in West Africa, Australasia, Latin America, the Caribbean and United States. A total of twenty-one Boeing 757-200s and ten 767-200s have been delivered to date, the majority with extended range capabilities.

The livery illustrated by Boeing 767-204 G-BKPW was unveiled during 1983 and represented an innovation in colourscheme design. Deep blue fuselage-length pinstripes begin at the belly and get gradually narrower as they approach the windowline, each trimmed with a combination of yellow and red. The white upper fuselage displays bold 'Britannia' titles, which compliment the fuselage colouring and appear alongside a representation of Queen Boadicea's helmeted head. On the tail, the famous British warrior-queen is reproduced as a full length motif, complete with Union flag shield, above a repetition of the fuselage pinstriping.

BRITISH AIRWAYS

British Airways was formed on April 1st 1972 through the merger of BOAC and BEA. Scheduled passenger services are operated throughout Britain and to major cities in Europe, the Middle and Far East, Africa, Australasia, Latin America, the United States and Canada. Although based at London Heathrow, the carrier also maintains a strong presence at Gatwick airport, brought about by its acquisition of British Caledonian Airways and Dan Air in recent times. Other divisions operate from Birmingham and Manchester and within Scotland. Domestic and regional services are also flown by commuter affiliates Brymon Aviation and Cityflyer Express, with international partners including TAT European Airlines and USAir.

British Airways has mostly standardised on Boeing equipment with notable exceptions including ten Airbus Industrie A320-100/200s and seven McDonnell Douglas DC-10-30s inherited from British Caledonian, plus the irreplaceable fleet of seven BAC/SNIAS Concordes. The current fleet includes 737-400s, 747-100/200/400s, 757-200s and 767-300/ERs, with most 737-200s now operated by regional divisions at Birmingham, Gatwick and Manchester. British Aerospace is now only represented by thirteen turboprop ATPs serving in Scotland and by a small fleet of 1-11s operated in association with Maersk Air from Birmingham. Additional 747-400s and 767-300/ERs are on order, with 777-200s to be added from September 1995.

The livery illustrated by Airbus Industrie A320-211 G-BUSJ was officially unveiled on December 4th 1984. Created by Walter Landor Associates, it brings together pearl grey and royal blue to colour the entire fuselage and fin, joined by a bright red 'speedwing' beneath the windowline. The top half of the fin displays a small coat of arms above a quartered Union flag. All members of the fleet wear the same livery except for the supersonic Concordes, which must always be painted predominantly white for heat reflection purposes.

BRITISH ASIA AIRWAYS

British Asia Airways was created by British Airways in 1993 to operate services between London and Taiwan on behalf of the national carrier.

A single Boeing 747-400, delivered in March 1993, is used exclusively on the twice-weekly schedule between Heathrow and Taipei, routing via Hong Kong.

The livery is based on the fuselage colouring of British Airways with a large red Dragon motif displayed on a blue painted fin. The oriental image is further promoted by the use of Chinese-style 'British Asia Airways' lettering, which is reproduced on the forward cabin roof.

BRITISH MIDLAND

British Midland can trace its history back to the formation of a company known as Air Schools in 1938, which specialised in flying tuition. This led to the creation of Derby Aviation in 1949 (later Derby Airways), which then became known as British Midland Airways in 1964. Scheduled services were introduced in 1953 and these now link London-Heathrow and East Midlands with points throughout the United Kingdom and Europe. Inclusive-tour charters are also flown from East Midlands to holiday resorts in the Mediterranean. Airlines of Britain Holdings, in which SAS has a 24.9% stake, was formed in March 1987 to act as a holding company for British Midland and its subsidiaries - including Loganair and Manx Airlines.

British Midland is currently equipped with five 737-300s, six 737-400s, seven 737-500s, five McDonnell Douglas DC-9-10s and eight DC-9-30s, with the first of four ordered Fokker 100s having entered service during the summer of 1994. The carrier has also ordered five Fokker 70s and made arrangements to lease a further seven 737-500s from SAS, which will start to replace older DC-9s from 1995. Two Jetstream 41s are used on 'thinner' routes connecting East Midlands with Brussels and Edinburgh.

The livery illustrated by Fokker 100 G-BVJA was introduced in its original form on October 14th 1985, with a narrow red pinstripe being added to the design in early 1994 to help separate the two fuselage colours of blue and pale grey. Red 'BM' initials are displayed on the cabin roof and fin, together with a pale blue diamond motif, with British Midland titles appearing in white.

Britannia

BRITISH AIRWAYS
G-BUSJ

British Asia Airways
英
亞

BM British Midland
G-BVJA
BM

BRITISH WORLD AIRWAYS

British World Airways can trace its history back to January 1963 when two established cross-channel airlines, Channel Air Bridge and Silver City Airways, were merged to form British United Air Ferries. The airline was known as British Air Ferries from September 1967, with the present title being adopted in 1993 to coincide with a major image change. The activities of British World Airways remain as diverse as ever, ranging from holiday charter flights to ad-hoc and contract passenger and freight charters, although a scheduled service connecting Stansted with Bucharest has now been discontinued.

The Vickers Viscount, for many years the fleet mainstay, still remains in everyday use with the airline. The ten-strong fleet is mostly engaged in mail and newspaper contract flying but also supports the oil industry off the Scottish coast. Holiday charters are operated by a fleet of five British Aerospace 1-11s, supplemented by three 146-300s. British World also operates trooping flights under contract to the Ministry of Defence with the BAe 146 fleet.

The livery illustrated by British Aerospace 146-300 G-BRAB has been adopted by all types operated, including some of the Viscounts. The centrepiece of the design is a rampant silver lion motif, which is also reproduced on the fin over an extended burgundy coloured backdrop. Burgundy has also been used to colour 'British World' titles, the positioning of which varies between types. It should also be noted that two Viscounts wear full 'Parcel Force' markings, featuring red overall fuselage and fin colouring, for contract work on behalf the Post Office.

BWIA INTERNATIONAL

BWIA International was formed on January 1st 1980 as the result of a decision by the Trinidad and Tobago Government to merge its international and domestic carriers, BWIA (British West Indian Airways) and TTAS (Trinidad and Tobago Air Services) in the interests of efficiency; BWIA had been formed in November 1939 and TTAS had been operating since June 1974. The national airline of Trinidad and Tobago now operates scheduled international to points in Europe and North America, as well as regionally within the Caribbean.

A fleet of nine McDonnell Douglas MD-83s is kept busy on regional routes connecting Port of Spain with Antigua, Barbados, Georgetown, Grenada, Kingston, Miami, New York, Saint Lucia, Saint Maarten, Tobago and Toronto. Four Lockheed TriStar-500s fly the long haul services to Frankfurt, London and Zurich in Europe, in addition to supplementing the smaller MD-83s on higher density routes to New York and Toronto etc.

BWIA's livery was clearly designed to capture the atmosphere of the Caribbean, taking its inspiration from the golden sands which colour the fuselage and fin in the form of an expanding cheatline, neatly trimmed with a splash of Caribbean blue. The tail motif is a similarly coloured representation of the sun, with superimposed 'BWIA' lettering in magenta. The cabin roof accommodates full 'BWIA International' titling in magenta and black respectively, followed by the national flag and legend 'We are the Caribbean'.

CALEDONIAN AIRWAYS

Caledonian Airways was created on December 10th 1987 to assume the combined charter activities of British Caledonian Airways and British Airtours. Based at London Gatwick, the airline operates holiday charters to points in the Mediterranean, North and East Africa, the Canary Islands, Caribbean and North America.

The fleet currently includes four ex British Airways Lockheed TriStars, six Boeing 757-200s and two ex-BCAL McDonnell Douglas DC-10-30s.

The livery of Caledonian Airways, illustrated by Lockheed TriStar-100 G-BBAJ, is based on the fuselage colouring of British Airways, whilst retaining the goodwill of the Caledonian name and motif. The red 'speed wing' of British Airways has been replaced by a delicate gold cheatline, which starts at the nose, although the midnight blue and pearl grey fuselage colouring is identical to facilitate the interchange of aircraft between the two fleets. Caledonian titles are reproduced in the same optima typeface as British Airways, with the family resemblance further enhanced by the application of blue painted engine housings.

CANADIAN AIRLINES INTERNATIONAL

Canadian Airlines International was formed on April 26th 1987 as the result of a merger between Canadian Pacific Airlines and Pacific Western Airlines, both of which had long and illustrious histories. Today, the airline maintains a comprehensive domestic route system with scheduled international connections serving cities in Europe, the Far East, Australasia, Latin America and the United States.

Domestically, the carrier continues to depend heavily on a fleet of around fifty Boeing 737-200s, supplemented since October 1991 by a growing number of Airbus Industrie A320-200s and high capacity Boeing 767-300/ERs on major domestic trunk routes. Local feeder services are also provided by several 'Canadian Partner' airlines. The Boeing 767-300/ERs, of which twelve are operated, also provide service to Frankfurt, London, Manchester, Milan and Rome in Europe, and to Mexico City and Honolulu from Toronto. Three Boeing 747-400s serve on Pacific routes to Bangkok, Hong Kong and Tokyo-Narita, supplemented by McDonnell Douglas DC-10-30s on services to Hawaii and beyond.

The livery adopted by Canadian Airlines International, illustrated by Boeing 747-475 C-GMWW, was based on a relatively new Canadian Pacific design and modified to incorporate Pacific Western's red wing motif. In using a combination of midnight blue, bright red and 'pewter' to colour the fuselage and fin, the airline has played down its national identity in favour of a more businesslike image. The five expanded tail bars represent the five continents served by the airline and the 'Canadi>n' titles have been arranged as such to overcome Canada's controversial bi-lingual laws, allowing for interpretation in French or English without the need for separate translations.

ITISH WORLD

BWIA
We are the Caribbean
Tri Star 500
BWIA

CALEDONIAN

CATHAY PACIFIC AIRWAYS

Although privately owned by Swire Pacific Ltd. and the Hong Kong and Shanghai Bank, Cathay Pacific is recognised as the flag carrier of the British Crown Colony of Hong Kong. The company was formed in September 1946 to operate war-surplus Douglas DC-3s on regional passenger and cargo charter flights, with the first scheduled services introduced in 1948. Today, Cathay Pacific's all-jet fleet connects Hong Kong with twenty-six other major cities in the Asia-Pacific region, plus thirteen other points in Africa, the Middle East, Europe and North America. Scheduled all-cargo services are also flown by a fleet of dedicated Boeing 747F freighters.

Cathay Pacific is currently equipped with a fleet of six Lockheed TriStars (to be phased out by August 1996), eight Boeing 747-200s, three 747-200Fs, six 747-300s, twenty 747-400s and two 747-400Fs. The airline has also ordered ten Airbus Industrie A330-300s (1995 to 1996), six A340-300s (1996 to 1997) and eleven Boeing 777-200s (1996 to 1998). In the meantime, the carrier will lease four new A340-200s from Airbus/Philippine Airlines (first delivery October 1994) and one 747-400 from International Lease Finance Corp. (from May 1995), to facilitate route expansion.

The livery illustrated by Boeing 747-467 VR-HOP has represented Cathay Pacific for several decades, dating back to the pre-widebodied era when Boeing 707s and Convair 880s were the fleet mainstay. Although it will still be seen for some time, from September 1994 the carrier will begin to phase in a new image that will ultimately be adopted fleetwide.

CONDOR

Condor is a wholly owned subsidiary of the German national airline, Lufthansa. Formed during October 1961 as a result of the merger of two earlier Lufthansa subsidiaries, Deutsche Flugdienst and Condor Luftreederei, the company now offers a range of scheduled and inclusive tour charter flights to major holiday destinations in the Mediterranean, the Canary Islands, Africa, the Far East and North America, from cities throughout Germany. Scheduled destinations include Fuerteventura, Funchal, Grand Canaria, Lanzarote, Mahe Island (Seychelles), Mauritius, Palma de Mallorca and Tenerife.

The present Condor fleet consists of eighteen Boeing 757-200s, seven 767-300/ERs (with another four to be added by 1995) and three McDonnell Douglas DC-10-30s. The airline also operates four Boeing 737-300s leased from Germania. Note: A Lufthansa Boeing 747-400 is currently being operated in full Condor markings on services to Taiwan. Similarly, a Condor 767-300/ER is now being operated in full Lufthansa markings on services to Australia.

Condor's livery, illustrated by Boeing 757-230 D-ABNX, is similar in many respects to that of Lufthansa. Both carriers have adopted white and grey fuselage colouring and display titles in the same position (forward cabin roof), colour (blue) and typeface (Helvetica). In addition to emphasising Lufthansa's involvement in Condor, it also eases the transfer of aircraft between the two fleets. By simply reversing the blue and yellow tail colours of Lufthansa, Condor has not only distinguished itself from the national carrier but also adopted a colour that is perhaps very fitting for a holiday airline. The final touch is provided by a stylised bird motif which, although being very similar to the flying crane of Lufthansa, is different enough to provide Condor with its very own corporate identity.

CONTINENTAL AIRLINES

Houston, Texas-based Continental Airlines can trace its history back over fifty years to the formation of Varney Speed Lines in 1937. An extensive domestic route system, radiating from major traffic hubs at Denver, Houston, Newark and Cleveland, is complimented by the feeder connections of 'Continental Express' and by a new in-house, low-fare operation known as CALite. The carrier also flies internationally to points in Canada, Mexico, South America, Australasia, the Far East and Europe.

For domestic and trans-border operations Continental Airlines is equipped with a large narrowbodied fleet of Boeing 727-200s, 737-100/200/300s and McDonnell Douglas DC-9-30/MD-82s, supplemented by higher capacity Airbus Industrie A300B4s and McDonnell Douglas DC-10-10s on popular trunk routes. However, the older types are now beginning to be phased out as deliveries of fifty ordered Boeing 737-500s and twenty-five 757-200s gain momentum. The carrier has also ordered twelve Boeing 767-300/ERs and five 777-200/ERs to replace its existing long haul fleet, which currently includes two 747-100s, three 747-200s and thirteen McDonnell Douglas DC-10-30s.

The focal point of Continental's latest livery, introduced in February 1991, is a three dimensional globe motif, which features lines of latitude and longitude in white and gold respectively, set against a deep blue backdrop. White upper and grey lower fuselage colouring is joined by a gold pinstripe fractionally above wing level, with blue Continental titles displayed on the cabin roof. Note: one DC-10-30 is now wearing full Alitalia markings on one side of its fuselage promote a new code-sharing agreement between Continental and the Italian carrier. Another three or four aircraft, including some belonging to Alitalia, will eventually adopt a joint livery to supplant the dual identity approach.

CROATIA AIRLINES

Croatia Airlines was formed in 1989 and commenced international operations with a leased McDonnell Douglas MD-80. Scheduled services now connect the capital, Zagreb, with Amsterdam, Berlin, Bratislava, Brussels, Copenhagen, Dubrovnik, Frankfurt, London, Moscow, Munich, Paris, Prague, Pula, Rome, Skopje, Split, Tirana, Vienna and Zurich.

The carrier is currently equipped with five ex-Lufthansa Boeing 737-200s and two turboprop ATR42-300s. However, future plans call for the introduction of leased Boeing 767 equipment for use on services to North America, including Toronto.

The livery illustrated by Boeing 737-230 9A-CTA is displayed by all fleet members, including the two ATR42s. Blue underside colouring is contrasted by a white cabin exterior, which promotes the Croatia Airlines name in black uppercase lettering alongside the carrier's chequered motif, which is red and white. The theme is continued on the fin, but with the motif leading from a blue wedge. The Croatian flag plays only a small part in the design, appearing alongside the registration markings on the upper rear part of the fuselage.

CATHAY PACIFIC

Condor
D-ABNX

Continental

CROATIA AIRLINES
9A-CTA
TA
STOP

CROSSAIR

Crossair was formed on February 14th 1975 as Business Flyers Basle Ltd. and adopted the present title some three and a half years later to promote a more international image. As a regional subsidiary of Swissair, the airline now provides scheduled passenger services connecting Zurich, Basle and Geneva with points throughout the European Community.

Crossair is equipped with a total of twenty-nine Saab 340A/Bs, five leased Fokker 50s, three leased British Aerospace 146-300s and four Avroliner RJ85s. The leased aircraft will leave the fleet as new Saab 2000s are introduced, twenty of which have been ordered for delivery between 1995 and 1997. These are also expected to replace the original fourteen Saab 340As, eight of which have been leased to other carriers - including its Business Air subsidiary.

The livery illustrated by Avroliner RJ85 HB-IXH was designed to promote Switzerland's entry into the European Community, its unveiling coinciding with the introduction of new Avroliner RJ85 equipment. Using the familiar corporate colours of red, white and blue, the livery represents Switzerland (red) joining the EC (blue) in the form of expanding brush strokes, with the Swiss representation becoming larger with each repetition. The tail, as always, accommodates the Swiss national flag, with 'Crossair' titles appearing in blue on the cabin roof.

CSA CZECHOSLOVAK AIRLINES

CSA can trace its history back to July 1923 with its foundation as Czechoslovenske Statni Aerolinie. Operations began on October 28th between Prague and Bratislava using ex-military A-14 bi-planes. International services were inaugurated in 1930 and soon encompassed much of Europe. After a six year suspension of operations during the Second World War, the present CSA was formed on September 15th 1945 through the merger of the pre-war CSA (Ceskoslovenska Letecka Spolecnost) and Sovenska Letecka Akciova Spolecnost. Today, the airline provides scheduled international services connecting Prague with cities throughout Europe, and to points in North America, the Middle and Far East, North Africa and Australasia.

CSA has progressively rolled over many of the Soviet types previously operated and replaced them with a combination of ATR72s (four), Boeing 737-500s (five) and Airbus Industrie A310-300s (two) acquired in the west. The airline continues to operate four Tupolev Tu-154Ms, five Tu-134As and a recently reduced fleet of three Ilyushin Il-62Ms.

After experimenting with at least two different liveries in an effort to update the previous OK-Jet image, CSA eventually adopted the design illustrated by Tupolev Tu-154M OK-TCD in April 1992. Welcoming the new ATR72s and 737-500s to the fleet, it was the first design to completely lose the 'OK' initials that had been in use since the delivery of the airline's first Tupolev Tu-134 in December 1971. Precedence is now given to red 'CSA' lettering, which is displayed on the forward cabin above secondary 'Czechoslovak Airlines' titles in white. A delicate blue and red cheatline arrangement separates the white and grey fuselage colouring at wing level, with the tail featuring a stylish representation of the Czech flag.

CUBANA

Cubana was founded in 1930 and commenced operations with a single Ford Trimotor. From humble beginnings the Cuban carrier has developed an international network that now reaches Africa and Europe, as well as several major cities throughout North, Central and South America and the Caribbean region. Domestic services are also undertaken, together with international passenger and freight charters.

Cuba's close relationship with the former Soviet Union is reflected in the composition of the Cubana fleet, which includes Antonov An-24/26s and Yakovlev Yak-40/42s for domestic and regional operations, Tupolev Tu-154s for medium-haul flights and Ilyushin Il-62Ms for long haul or high capacity sectors. Antonov An-2s and Mil Mi-8 helicopters are also used locally, with additional cargo capacity provided by two Ilyushin Il-76 freighters. A McDonnell Douglas DC-10-30 is operated in association with AOM French Airlines on services connecting Havana with Paris and Madrid, and eight Fokker F.27 Friendships are being acquired during the summer of 1994 to replace An-24s domestically.

The livery illustrated by Yakovlev Yak-42D CU-T1279 was introduced in its original form during 1970 and has stood the test of time extremely well. Its focal point is a stylised national flag, which colours the tail in such a way that twin red cheatlines flow into the design very comfortably. 'Cubana' titles appear in dark blue and are succeeded by the national flag on the upper forward fuselage. The white painted underside has given the livery something of a 'face lift' in recent times, although several aircraft continue to wear a grey underside.

CYPRUS AIRWAYS

The tiny Mediterranean island of Cyprus employs a modern international flag carrier to connect it points throughout Europe and the Middle East. Scheduled passenger services currently link Larnaca with Amman, Amsterdam, Athens, Bahrain, Beirut, Berlin, Birmingham, Brussels, Cairo, Damascus, Dubai, Frankfurt, Jeddah, Kuwait, Linz, London, Manchester, Munich, Paris, Riyadh, Rome, Salzburg, Tel Aviv, Thessaloniki, Vienna and Zurich. Charter services are now the responsibility of a separate subsidiary, created in 1990 under the name of Eurocypria Airlines.

A fleet almost completely standardised on Airbus Industrie equipment includes eight A320-200s (including three leased to Eurocypria) and four A310-200s. The airline continues to employ three 94-seat British Aerospace 1-11-500s on routes to the Middle East, Greece and Italy.

The livery illustrated by Airbus Industrie A310-203 5B-DAR utilises shades of gold and blue to colour the cheatlines and tail. The company motif of a winged mountain goat, known as the Mouflon, is accommodated in the lower half of the fin in white on blue, with blue 'Cyprus Airways' titling displayed on the cabin roof.

crossair
HB-IXF

CSA
CZECHOSLOVAK AIRLINES
OK-TCD

CU-T1279
CUBANA
YAK-42D

CYPRUS AIRWAYS
5B-DAR
A310

DELTA AIR LINES

Atlanta-based Delta Air Lines was originally formed in 1924 as a humble crop dusting concern under the name of Huff Daland Dusters, flying crop-spraying aircraft in Mississippi during the summer months and transferring the whole operation to Peru for the winter. A mail service was inaugurated in 1927 between Peru and Ecuador, leading to a name change in 1928 to Delta Air Service. The present title was adopted in 1945 as the carrier began to build an extensive passenger and freight network within the United States, later spreading into Canada, Mexico and the Caribbean and more recently into Europe and the Far East. Domestic services are flown from five major hubs and embrace the entire US mainland, with additional regional feeder flights provided by Atlantic Southeast Airlines, Business Express, Comair and SkyWest under the marketing name of 'Delta Connection'.

A vast fleet currently includes aircraft from four different manufacturers, namely Airbus Industrie (A310-300 - soon to be phased out), Boeing (727-200, 737-200/300, 757-200, 767-200/300/ER), Lockheed (TriStar) and McDonnell Douglas (MD-88 and MD-11). A major fleet renewal program is already well advanced and will eventually see remaining JT8D-powered 727/737-200s replaced by new 737-300s and MD-90s, which are on order.

The company name was originally taken from the Mississippi Delta and is illustrated by a large blue and red delta, affectionately known as the 'widget', on the fin and forward fuselage areas. A dark blue windowline, which originates from the black anti-dazzle panel, is separated from black 'Delta' titling by a full length narrow red pinstripe. Although the lower fuselage is finished in natural metal or pale grey, a broad band of white follows the contour of the cheatline down to wing level. 'Delta' titles are repeated on the tail in white on blue and also accompany a smaller motif on the engine housings.

EGYPTAIR

Egyptair can trace its history back to June 7th 1932 when the British company Airwork Ltd. entered into an agreement with the Misr Bank of Cairo to form Misr Airwork. Domestic operations commenced in July 1933 with a small fleet of de Havilland DH.84 Dragons, with the first international connections following in 1934. Airwork withdrew its interest in 1949 and the airline became known simply as Misrair. The carrier was known as United Arab Airlines from 1960 and adopted its present title on October 10th 1971. Today, Egyptair provides scheduled international connections to major cities in Africa, Europe, the Middle and Far East and North America, with domestic flights linking Cairo, Luxor, Abu Simbel, Alexandria, Aswan, Hurghada, Luxor, New Valley, Ras Al Khaima and Sharm el Sheik.

Egyptair has now rolled over most of the Boeing 737-200s delivered during the mid-seventies and replaced them with a mix of Boeing 737-500s (five) and Airbus Industrie A320-200s (seven). Three 767-200s are used mostly on services within Africa, with two longer range 767-300/ERs providing 'thinner' transatlantic capacity. Airbus Industrie A300B4s (five) and A300-600Rs (nine) fly major trunk routes to Europe, the Middle East and North Africa with two 747-300s serving Bangkok, Manila, New York, Tokyo and Paris.

Egyptair took the opportunity to update its image prior to the introduction of several new aircraft types from May 1990. The focal point of the design continues to be a representation of Horus, the omnipotent Falcon-headed god of ancient Egypt, which is now embraced by an upward extension of the familiar red and gold cheatline arrangement. Titles, which appear in English and Arabic, are now red instead of black (likewise for the registration lettering) and continue to be separated by the Egyptian flag. Finally, natural metal or grey coloured fuselage undersides have been substituted for a white overall appearance.

EL AL ISRAEL AIRLINES

El Al was formed in November 1948 as the national carrier of the new state of Israel and commenced operations the following year using a Douglas DC-4 on routes to Europe. Today, the airline connects Tel Aviv with cities in North and East Africa, Europe, the Far East and North America. Scheduled all-cargo services are managed by a separate subsidiary known simply as CAL-Cargo Air Lines.

Most routes to Europe and Africa are served by a fleet of seven Boeing 757-200s, supplemented by two 737-200s on thinner sectors and six 747-200s on major trunk routes to Amsterdam and London. Four 767-200s (including two ERs) serve Beijing and Warsaw, in addition to crossing the Atlantic to points in Canada and the United States. The 747-200s also serve cities in North America and the Far East, with two recently acquired 747-400s (another on order) providing nonstop service to North America. A further three 747s are configured as freighters and operated by CAL.

The fresh white fuselage is dissected by an unusual cheatline arrangement, which starts at the nose in bright blue and later changes to a darker shade with a tapered joint. The brighter shade later expands at an angle above the windowline to ultimately colour the tail fin, which is topped by the Israeli flag. In its complete form, as illustrated by Boeing 747-458 4X-ELA, the two shades of blue are also wrapped around the engine housings. Dual language titling appears on the forward upper fuselage with El Al displayed in bright blue English lettering, interspersed with the Hebrew equivalent in the darker shade.

EMIRATES AIRLINES

Emirates Airlines commenced operations over a regional network on October 25th 1985 using a Boeing 737-300 and an Airbus Industrie A300B4 leased from Pakistan International Airlines. Today, the carrier provides scheduled international connections linking Dubai with Amman, Bangkok, Beirut, Bombay, Cairo, Colombo, Damascus, Delhi, Dhahran, Dhaka, Doha, Frankfurt, Hong Kong, Istanbul, Jakarta, Jeddah, Karachi, Kuwait, Larnaca, London (some flights via Abu Dhabi), Male, Manchester, Manila, Muscat, Paris, Riyadh, Rome, Singapore, Tehran and Zurich.

A modern fleet of Airbus Industrie A300-600s and A310-300s is supplemented by three Boeing 727-200s, which are used exclusively on services to Beirut, Doha and Male, and at off peak times to Istanbul and Kuwait. With long haul expansion in mind, Emirates Airlines has ordered seven Boeing 777s, four of which will be configured for extended range operations.

The livery chosen by Emirates Airlines, illustrated by Airbus Industrie A310-308 A6-EKI, was designed to promote a bold national identity and features a stylised United Arab Emirates flag as its centrepiece, complimented by gold 'Emirates' titling in English and Arabic respectively. The airline's gold coloured motif appears as a secondary feature of the design and is only displayed on the engine housings.

DELTA
DELTA

EGYPTAIR
مصر للطيران

EL AL

Emirates
الامارات
A310-300
A6-EKI

ETHIOPIAN AIRLINES

Based in the capital, Addis Ababa, Ethiopian Airlines was founded by decree of Emperor Haile Selassie in December 1945 to upgrade the country's international and domestic air services. Today, the company is one of Africa's leading air carriers with a reputation for service and punctuality that is admired throughout the continent. In addition to serving more than forty domestic points, the majority unable to sustain jet service, Ethiopian Airlines also flies to several points throughout Africa and to Abu Dhabi, Aden, Athens, Bangkok, Beijing, Berlin, Bombay, Dubai, Frankfurt, Jeddah, Karachi, London, Muscat, Riyadh, Rome and Sanaa.

For scheduled international passenger operations the Ethiopian national carrier is equipped with a modern all-Boeing fleet, including one 737-200, four 757-200s and three 767-200/ERs. These aircraft are also used on domestic trunk routes, with five DHC-6 Twin Otter 300s, one DHC-5D Buffalo and two ATR42s connecting smaller communities. In addition, a cargo division is equipped with two Lockheed L.100-30s and one Boeing 757-200PF, and also makes use of the Buffalo as and when required.

The livery illustrated by Boeing 767-260/ER ET-AIF has all the classic features of a 'fifties design, with its attractive tail emblem representing three tail feathers in the national colours of green, yellow and red. A similarly coloured and intricate cheatline begins with a bright red lightning bolt at the cockpit windows, which also provides a backdrop for the company's rampant lion motif in yellow. Red 'Ethiopian' titling is displayed in English and Amharic with the national language appearing nearest the nose on both sides.

EVA AIR

EVA Air was formed in 1989 as a subsidiary of the Evergreen Group of Companies and initiated scheduled services on July 1st 1991 with two newly delivered Boeing 767-300/ERs. These are now flown from Taipei and Kaohsiung (Taiwan's second largest city) to Auckland, Bangkok, Dubai, Ho Chi Minh City, Honolulu, Jakarta, Kuala Lumpur, London-Gatwick, Los Angeles, Manila, New York-Newark, Paris, Penang, Phuket Island, San Francisco, Seattle, Singapore, Sydney and Vienna, with the Maldive Islands served on a charter basis. Scheduled all-cargo services will also be introduced from late 1994.

A modern all-widebodied fleet currently includes eight Boeing 747-400s, four 767-200s and five 767-300/ERs. Six McDonnell Douglas MD-11s (including three freighters) have been ordered for delivery between August 1994 and December 1995.

EVA Air was originally proposed under the Evergreen name and only adopted its present title following objections from Evergreen International of the United States. This is reflected in the carrier's livery, illustrated by Boeing 747-45E B-16401, which is predominantly green in colour and also includes secondary 'Evergreen Group' titling. A white cabin exterior provides a clean backdrop for EVA Air titles in green uppercase lettering (repeated in Chinese) above which appears a green, orange tipped fuselage stripe. The tail motif adheres to the shipping interests of the Evergreen Group and features a green compass star within a cropped globe, with lines of latitude and longitude reproduced in orange. The remainder of the fin is painted green, with orange trimming the trailing edge.

EXCALIBUR AIRWAYS

Excalibur Airways was created from the assets of Trans European Airways (UK), which ceased operations in late 1991 following the failure of its Belgian parent. Using a new fleet of Airbus Industrie A320-200s (leased from the GPA Group), the fledgling charter airline launched operations from London-Gatwick and Manchester on May 1st 1992, flying to holiday destinations in the Mediterranean, North Africa and the Middle East. Today, the carrier also flies from Birmingham and East Midlands.

Four 180-seat Airbus Industrie A320-200s form the nucleus of the fleet, supplemented by a smaller Boeing 737-300; the latter being introduced during the summer '94 season for use on 'thinner' charter routes to Italy.

The Excalibur name is graphically portrayed in the form of a stylised sword, on which the titles and tail motif are based. A white cabin exterior plays host to mauve Excalibur titling, which is ingeniously arranged to represent a sword with the help of a small accompanying tip. The tail motif focuses on the handle of the sword and appears in white over a mauve coloured backdrop. The sword of Excalibur originates from English folklore and the legendary tales of King Arthur of Camelot, in which the sword was set in stone and could only be retrieved by its rightful owner. All aircraft wear the livery illustrated by Boeing 737-3Q8 G-OCHA.

FEDERAL EXPRESS-FEDEX

Memphis-based Federal Express was formed in 1971 and commenced operations two years later with a fleet of Dassault Falcon 20 'freighters'. Following CAB deregulation of air cargo in November 1977 the carrier received authority to operate larger aircraft and a fleet of Boeing 727 and McDonnell Douglas DC-10 aircraft was progressively assembled. International operations were greatly expanded following the acquisition of Flying Tigers on August 7th 1989. Now the world's largest express transport company, Federal Express serves over 180 countries - including destinations in Africa, Asia, Australasia, Europe, the Middle East, and North and South America.

A large fleet includes over fifty Boeing 727-100Fs, ninety 727-200Fs, six Boeing 747-200Fs (soon to be phased out), eleven McDonnell Douglas DC-10-10Fs, nineteen DC-10-30Fs and thirteen MD-11Fs. In addition, twenty-five Airbus Industrie A300-600Fs will be delivered new between 1994 and 1998 and thirteen A310-200 freighter conversions are being acquired from Lufthansa between 1994/1995. A fleet of over two hundred Cessna Cargomasters and thirty-two Fokker Friendships is operated by several smaller regional operators throughout the United States.

Federal Express officially adopted the FedEx identity on June 23rd 1994 and at the same time unveiled a new visual image, illustrated by Airbus Industrie A310-203F N407FE. The new livery, which uses more dynamic shades of the trademark purple and orange colouring, incorporates the legend 'The World on Time' as well as secondary 'Federal Express' titling. The change will be reflected on thirty undelivered widebodies joining the fleet over the next three to four years, and on all new ground support vehicles. Most of the aircraft will be Airbus Industrie A300-600s and A310-300s, plus some McDonnell Douglas DC-10s. The new livery will be adopted by existing aircraft and vehicles as part of the routine maintenance schedule.

ETHIOPIAN
ET-AIF

EVA AIR
空航榮長

EXCALIBUR
G-OCHA

FedEx
N407FE
FedEx
Federal Express
The World On Time
FedEx

FINNAIR

The national flag carrier of Finland can trace its history back to November 1st 1923 when it was formed as Aero OY to connect several domestic points using a Junkers F.13 seaplane. Today, the carrier offers extensive passenger and freight services to destinations throughout Europe, and to North America and the Far East. A comprehensive domestic network is also maintained.

A modern all-jet fleet is mostly standardised on McDonnell Douglas equipment, although two ex-Kar Air Airbus Industrie A300B4s have been added in recent times. Five different members of the DC-9/MD-80 family, including five DC-9-41s, twelve DC-9-51s, nine MD-82s, five MD-83s and three MD-87s, provide short to medium capacity, with four MD-11s and five DC-10-30s (some leased out) equipping the long haul fleet.

Finnair's livery, illustrated by McDonnell Douglas MD-11 OH-LGB, dates back to a period when flags were commonly used as a key identifying feature. On all types, a royal blue windowline is worn over an all-white (or white upper and grey lower) fuselage, with the tail painted to represent the national flag. Traditional 'Finnair' titles appear on the cabin roof, whilst the corporate motif (a white 'F' in a blue disk) is discreetly displayed near the nose. A smart fuselage sash in three shades of blue is worn only by members of the MD-80 family.

GARUDA INDONESIAN AIRWAYS

The national flag carrier of Indonesia, Garuda was formed on March 31st 1950 to replace its short lived predecessor, Indonesian Airways, which had been based in Rangoon (Burma) during the nation's fight for independence. The company now provides vital airlinks between the numerous Indonesian islands as well as offering scheduled services throughout the Far East and to points in Australasia, Africa, the Middle East, Europe and North America.

Having transferred many of its domestic routes to subsidiary Merpati Nusantara Airlines, Garuda's short haul interests are now confined to major trunk routes and its fleet strength has been reduced accordingly. A total of sixteen Boeing 737-400s have been ordered for delivery through 1997 and in the meantime Garuda is leasing eight 737-300s from ILFC. Regionally, the airline uses nine Airbus Industrie A300B4s (to be replaced by A330-300s between 1996 and 1997) and ten A300-600Rs. Additional capacity and range is provided by six McDonnell Douglas DC-10-30s, six MD-11s, seven Boeing 747-200s and two 747-400s (with a further seven to be delivered between 1995 and 1998).

Designed by Walter Landor Associates, the livery illustrated by Boeing 747-2U3B PK-GSC was unveiled in September 1985 and centres on a bird motif of Indonesian folklore, from which the company takes its name. The 'Garuda' bird is reproduced in shades of blue and turquoise and set against a dark blue fin, its wing feathers ingeniously arranged to represent the five national ideals. The motif also appears alongside black 'Garuda Indonesia' titles on a white coloured fuselage, with a small Indonesian flag displayed on the upper forward cabin.

GB AIRWAYS

GB Airways, formerly known as Gibair, and originally Gibraltar Airways, was formed by the Bland Group in 1931 to serve Gibraltar, a British Colony situated at the southern tip of Spain. Now 49% owned by British Airways, the airline provides regular scheduled services connecting London (Gatwick and Heathrow) and Manchester with Gibraltar. The airline also serves Funchal, Marrakech and Tunis from Gatwick; Casablanca from Heathrow; and Tangier from Heathrow and Manchester. Charters are also flown to points in Europe and the Mediterranean area.

GB Airways is currently equipped with four ex-British Airways Boeing 737-200s, although two additional aircraft have been leased for operation by its GB Leisure affiliate.

The focal point of the GB Airways livery is the red diamond motif of the Bland Group, which is displayed on the fin and forward fuselage within bands of blue and red. The positioning of the motif at the front of the cabin provides both a starting point and change of direction for the dual coloured cheatlines, which connect under the forward fuselage in the form of a 'smile'. Titles are arranged in upper and lower case lettering and displayed on the cabin roof, with 'GB' in blue and 'airways' in red.

GHANA AIRWAYS

Ghana Airways was formed on July 4th 1958 by the Ghanaian Government and BOAC to take over the operations of West African Airways Corporation in the former British colony known as the Gold Coast. BOAC provided a Boeing Stratocruiser which, on July 16th, inaugurated the new airline's first service between Accra and London. The airline became fully operational on October 1st 1958 when it assumed the domestic and regional operations of WAAC. Today, the company provides all-jet services linking the capital Accra with Abidjan, Banjul, Conakry, Cotonou, Dusseldorf, Gran Canaria, Dakar, Freetown, Harare, Lagos, London and Rome.

Services to Europe and Harare in southern Africa are flown by a single McDonnell Douglas DC-10-30, with two Fokker F.28 Fellowships serving all other routes.

The livery illustrated by McDonnell Douglas DC-10-30 9G-ANA is based on the national flag and features a broad cheatline in the colours of the Ghanaian tricolour. The Ghana Airways emblem is carried on the centre engine, surmounted by a large representation of the flag, and repeated on the other engines. Fuselage titles appear in the black of the national star and are accompanied by a further flag. The Fokker Fellowships, which first introduced the livery in May 1974, wear an all-white finish with just a Ghanaian tail flag and standard fuselage lettering.

FINNAIR
MD-11

Garuda Indonesia
PK-GSC

GB airways
G-BGDB

GHANA AIRWAYS
9G-ANA
State of Qatar

GULF AIR

Gulf Air was originally formed in March 1950 as Gulf Aviation Co. Ltd. and commenced operations on July 5th using Avro Ansons. The present title was adopted in early 1973 and since April 1974 the carrier has been jointly owned by the Gulf States of Bahrain, Qatar, Oman and the United Arab Emirates. Scheduled passenger services fly to points throughout the Middle East and to East Africa, Asia, Australasia, Europe and North America.

Gulf Air is now nearing the end of a major fleet renewal program which has seen Boeing 737-200s and Lockheed TriStars replaced by twelve Airbus Industrie A320-200s and twenty Boeing 767-300/ERs. The carrier has also taken delivery of three A340-300s and has a further three on order for delivery between 1995 and 1996. Additional cargo capacity is provided by a leased Boeing 757-200PF, with a further two expected to added..

Gulf Air's livery, illustrated by Boeing 767-3P6/ER A40-GR, incorporates the national colours of Bahrain, Qatar, Oman and the United Arab Emirates in a design which is both stylish and inventive. An extended chin flash in maroon, green and red leads a white coloured fuselage, above which intricate gold lettering pronounces Gulf Air in English and Arabic respectively. The Golden Falcon motif, symbolic of the Arabian peninsula, confines vertical stripes of maroon, green and red to the top half of the fin, with gold coloured script used to clarify the bird of prey's identity below. The Golden Falcon also appears on the white painted engine housings of the newer generation fleet.

HAPAG LLOYD

Hapag Lloyd was formed in 1972 by the shipping group of the same name to operate passenger charters and inclusive tour flights from cities throughout Germany. The carrier flies to holiday destinations in the Mediterranean, the Canary Islands, Central and Eastern Europe and Africa. Bavaria-Germanair was absorbed in January 1979.

A modern fleet standardised on Boeing and Airbus Industrie equipment currently comprises nine 737-400s, five 737-500s, four A310-200s and three A310-300s.

The carrier's image, illustrated by Airbus Industrie A310-204 D-AHLZ, is very much that of the Hapag Lloyd group, with the parent company providing not only the dark blue 'HL' motif but also the colours of the livery as a whole. Twin blue and orange cheatlines are conventionally arranged, dissecting the fuselage which is pure white to wing level and grey thereafter. The theme is continued on the fin where the Hapag Lloyd motif appears in blue over a bright orange backdrop.

IBERIA

The national airline of Spain can trace its history back to July 7th 1940 with its formation as Linhas Aereas de Espana by the Spanish Government and Deutsche Lufthansa, eventually being nationalised on September 30th 1944. The present scheduled passenger and freight network is naturally comprehensive, linking all major Spanish cities with destinations in the Americas, Africa, the Middle East and Europe. Domestic services are also undertaken.

Long haul flights are currently served by seven Boeing 747-200Bs and eight McDonnell Douglas DC-10-30s, although eight Airbus Industrie A340-200s have been ordered for delivery between 1995 and 1997. Extensive modernisation of the short to medium fleet has seen Iberia add twenty-four McDonnell Douglas MD-87s and twenty-two Airbus Industrie A320-200s since 1990. These are now being joined by sixteen Boeing 757-200s, with older DC-9-30s and Boeing 727-200s soon to be phased out. Iberia has parked its fleet of eight A300B4s but may reactivate some of these aircraft as and when additional capacity is required. Deliveries of eight ordered A321-100s (due from 1994) have been deferred

A bright sunshine livery, illustrated by Boeing 747-256B EC-DNP, successfully combines the colours of the flag with a clue to the country's holiday attraction. Triple cheatlines in red, orange and yellow commence on the cabin roof behind the cockpit and sweep along the entire length of a white coloured fuselage as a window line. An ingenious 'IB' tail motif in red and yellow includes a small gold crown in honour of the country's monarchy, and the Iberia logo is carried in white on the fuselage and sometimes also in red on the engines.

ICELANDAIR

The Icelandic national airline was originally formed on June 3rd 1937 under the name of Flugfelag Akureyar and commenced operations using a single Waco floatplane between Akureyri and Reykjavik. Subsequent name changes occured in 1940 when it became known as Flugfelag Islands, followed by the present title in 1956. On August 1st 1973 the company was merged with Loftleidir Icelandic Airlines, which specialised in providing low fare North Atlantic travel. Today, Icelandair connects Reykjavik with ten domestic points and internationally with cities in Europe and North America.

A fleet of four Fokker 50s take care of domestic schedules and also connect Reykjavik with the Faroe Islands. A similar number of Boeing 737-400s serve Amsterdam, Copenhagen, Glasgow, Gothenburg, London, Oslo and Stockholm, with three Boeing 757-200s used mainly on North Atlantic routes connecting Reykjavik with Baltimore/Washington, Fort Lauderdale, New York and Orlando, plus Luxembourg, Salzburg and Zurich in Europe.

The focal point of Icelandair's international livery is unquestionably the blue coloured tail motif, which takes the form of a stylised 'F' on the port side but is mirrored on the other - as illustrated by Boeing 737-408 TF-FIA. This is complimented by a simple blue windowline, underscored by a similarly coloured pinstripe, which starts at the cockpit windows and continues in a conventional 'straight through' manner. Icelandair titles are reproduced in black upper case lettering on the cabin roof of the 737s and 757s, but on the Fokker 50s the Icelandic equivalent 'Flugleidir' is used. The domestic livery is also far more colourful in that it utilises the flag colours of blue, white and red.

GULFAIR
طيران الخليج
Golden Falcon

Hapag-Lloyd
A310-200

EC-DNP
IBERIA

ICELANDAIR

IRANAIR

The national airline of the Islamic Republic of Iran was formed in 1962 when the Government introduced a rationalisation policy and merged two existing independent companies, Persian Air Services and Iranian Airways. Services now link Tehran with cities in Europe, Asia and the Middle East, whilst also connecting the capital with several domestic communities. Iran Air Tours has been formed as a joint venture with Tajik Air and operates Tupolev Tu-154 equipment on charters reaching as far as northern Europe.

A US trade embargo has largely prevented IranAir from modernising the fleet that it built up during the 1970s and early '80s, which includes Boeing 707-320C, 727-100 and -200, 737-200, 747-100/200/200F/SP and Airbus Industrie A300B4 equipment. However, in more recent times the carrier has added six Fokker 100s for domestic operations and two A300-600Rs to supplement its international fleet.

By removing cheatlines and enlarging key recognition features such as titles and motifs, IranAir has successfully transformed an old and outdated image into a design that is both fresh and modern in appearance. Illustrated by Boeing 747SP-86 EP-IAD, the latest IranAir livery is based on a clean white backdrop with grey painted undersides and engine housings. Precedence is now given to dark blue IranAir lettering, which appears ahead of the national flag and secondary 'The Airline of the Islamic Republic of Iran' titling. The mythical 'Homa bird' motif, symbolising good fortune and great strength, continues to provide a classic tail motif but in a darker shade of blue and noticeably larger than before. The final touch is provided by a matching sweep of blue over the highest point of the fin, which appears in the same style and position as before.

ISTANBUL AIRLINES (ISTANBUL HAVA YOLLARI)

Istanbul Airlines was formed in December 1985 by joint Turkish and German interests and commenced operations the following year with a small fleet of Caravelles. Today, the airline operates passenger charters linking Istanbul, Adana, Ankara, Antalya, Dalaman and Izmir with points in Germany, Israel, Italy, the Netherlands, Spain and the United Kingdom. Contract cargo charters are also known to be operated between Istanbul and East Midlands.

The carrier is currently equipped with a fleet of seven Boeing 737-400s (all leased), seven 727-200s and one 727-200F freighter, with two 757-200s expected to be added in due course.

The livery illustrated by Boeing 737-4S3 TC-AVA is displayed by all fleet members with the exception of the 727-200F freighter - details of which appear below. A dark shade of blue has been used to colour the fin and fuselage underside, and also features in the pinstriping that reaches from nose to tail in a blue, red, blue arrangement. The tail motif portrays a stylised red tulip within a white enclosure, which is spherical and delicately outlined in blue. The significance of the tulip motif can be traced back to the ancient ottaman emperors, which considered the flower to be estimable. White also colours the upper reaches of the cabin, where red Istanbul Airlines titling is promoted. The Boeing 727-200F wears a similar livery but with large Istanbul CARGO wording, in red and blue respectively, displayed on a pale grey cabin exterior (without pinstriping or blue undersides).

JAL-JAPAN AIR LINES

Japan Air Lines was founded in 1951 and has grown to the point where it now operates one of the world's largest fleets of widebodied aircraft with a passenger and freight network serving cities in Europe, the Middle East, North, Central and South America, and numerous points throughout the Asia-Pacific region. In addition, the carrier also operates no less than one hundred and fifty domestic flights per day, connecting Tokyo with all major regional cities.

A total of eighty-eight Boeing 747s are currently in service or on order, including five -100s, twenty-one -200Bs, nine -200F freighters, thirteen -300s (including four SR models) and forty -400s (including ten 747-400Ds). The carrier is also equipped with three 767-200s, sixteen 767-300s and fourteen McDonnell Douglas DC-10-40s (seven configured for domestic use), with deliveries of ten ordered MD-11s currently in progress. Japan Air Lines has also ordered seven Boeing 737-400s (for delivery from May 1995) and ten 777-200s.

Designed by Walter Landor Associates and illustrated by Boeing 747-446 JA8077, the latest Japan Air Lines livery is based on a white cabin exterior, with pale grey colouring the lower body and engine housings. The most distinguishing feature of the design is a grey nose band, which culminates in a red square on the mid-forward fuselage section to highlight stylised JAL initials in black. Secondary Japan Airlines titling is also displayed on the cabin roof, alongside the more familiar JAL acronym. The traditional 'Tsuru' tail motif is formed by the outstretched wings of a red crane to symbolise a rising sun, and also incorporates white JAL initials in the new corporate style. The MD-11s have been named after rare Japanese birds and display a large J-Bird inscription on the raised engine, together with a portrayal of the featured bird on the winglets. A multi-coloured theme, consisting of birds and flowers, is also being adopted by a selection of Boeing 747-100/200s used exclusively on 'Super Resort Express' routes to Bangkok, Guam, Hawaii, Saipan and Australia.

JUST-JAPAN UNIVERSAL TRANSPORT SYSTEM

Japan Universal Transport System was created in 1991 as a joint venture between Japan Air Lines and Nippon Express and commenced scheduled domestic cargo operations in October of that year using a leased Boeing 747 freighter. The carrier has since added service to North America, in addition to supplementing the international network of JAL Cargo as and when required.

Japan Universal System Transport continues to employ a single Boeing 747-200F freighter for its domestic and international operations from Tokyo-Haneda.

The livery illustrated by Boeing 747-221F JA8160 was designed around the new image of Japan Air Lines, using the same white, red and grey colouring but in a completely different arrangement. A grey cheatline appears aft of the red square and accommodates secondary 'Japan Universal Air System' titles in black lettering. As with Japan Air Lines, the JUST acronym takes precedence and is displayed ahead of the cheatline in the same corporate style. A similar concept is adopted by all other JAL subsidiaries, including JAZ-Japan Air Charter and JTA-Japan Transocean Air, which also display variations of the white, grey and red 'family' theme. The tail motif is enclosed by red coloured bands and features a caricature of a whale.

IranAir
EP-IAD
AD

İstanbul Airlines
TC-AVA
BOEING 737-400
BOEING 737

JAL
JAL

Japan Universal System Transport
JUST

KENYA AIRWAYS

The collapse of the joint venture East African Airways in 1976 persuaded the Kenyan Government to form its own national flag carrier, to be responsible not only for providing international air links but also to connect several widespread domestic communities. International scheduled services commenced on January 22nd 1977 using Boeing 707s leased from British Midland Airways, and now connect Nairobi and Mombasa with points in Asia, Europe, the Middle East and Africa.

For domestic and regional routes Kenya Airways employs a fleet of three Fokker 50 turboprops and two leased Boeing 737-200s. Three Airbus Industrie A310-300s (including one leased from ILFC) are used on services to Bombay, Copenhagen, Dubai, Frankfurt, Karachi, London, Paris, Rome, Stockholm and Zurich, and also within Africa to Bujumbura, Dar-es-Salaam, Harare, Johannesburg and Kigali.

The livery of Kenya Airways, illustrated by Airbus Industrie A310-304 5Y-BFT, takes its colouring from the black, red and green of the national flag. A red 'straight through' cheatline appears directly below window level and is trimmed with black and green to complete the Kenyan tri-colour. Red is also used to colour Kenya Airways titling and the carrier's 'KA' motif, which can be found on the cabin roof and tail respectively, the latter within a black outlined enclosure.

KLM CITYHOPPER

KLM Cityhopper was originally formed as NLM in 1966 as a wholly-owned domestic subsidiary of the Dutch national carrier, KLM-Royal Dutch Airlines. International scheduled passenger services were inaugurated in April 1974 under the name of NLM Cityhopper, with the present title being adopted following a merger with Netherlines in April 1988. The carrier's scheduled network currently connects Amsterdam, Eindhoven, Maastricht and Rotterdam domestically, and with points in Belgium, France, Germany, Luxembourg, Sweden and the United Kingdom.

The carrier is equipped with a fleet of eleven Saab 340Bs, ten Fokker 50s and four 80-seat Fokker F.28-4000s.

The livery illustrated by F.28-4000 PH-CHD is worn by all fleet members and clearly distinguishes the Cityhopper division from its parent. A white cabin exterior is dissected by an extension of the tail colouring, which is lowered in line with the fin's leading edge to colour the entire rear fuselage section in a deep shade of blue. The Cityhopper name is displayed vertically in white lowercase lettering on the fin, and horizontally on the cabin roof in blue - where it is preceded by the KLM motif. Dutch and European Community flags are reproduced on the upper rear fuselage, a position favouring the Saab 340 and Fokker 50 aircraft but not so the Fellowships due to the location of the rear mounted engines.

KLM - ROYAL DUTCH AIRLINES

KLM has the distinction of being the oldest operating airline in the world, able to trace its history back to October 7th 1919. As the national airline of the Netherlands, KLM flies extensive scheduled passenger and freight services linking Amsterdam with more than 150 cities on six continents. The carrier also has financial interests in Air UK (14.9%), ALM Antillean Airlines (40%), Martinair Holland (29%), Northwest Airlines (22.3%) and Transavia Airlines (80%), with KLM Cityhopper being a wholly owned subsidiary.

A large all-jet fleet currently includes six Fokker 100s (leased), fifteen Boeing 737-300s, twelve 737-400s, ten Airbus Industrie A310-200s (to be phased out between late 1994 and 1996), twelve 747-200Bs, three 747-300s, sixteen 747-400s and six McDonnell Douglas MD-11s (with another four to be delivered by April 1997).The airline has also contracted to lease a minimum of seven Boeing 767-300/ERs from ILFC for delivery from June 1995, and is due to receive two ordered 747-400F freighters in August and September 1996.

The two shades of blue appearing in today's KLM livery have been used for nearly fifty years in various forms, with the lighter shade colouring the roof of all KLM aircraft since 1973. This continues to be supported by a darker coloured windowline and white underlying trim, below which the fuselage is painted pale grey. The crowned KLM motif is displayed on the fin in the lighter shade of blue, and also on the cabin roof in white. Winglets provide a further opportunity to promote the KLM name, as illustrated by McDonnell Douglas MD-11 PH-KCA.

KOREAN AIR

Korean Air was formed in 1962 to succeed Korean National Airlines (formed in 1948) as the South Korean flag carrier. Today, the airline flies scheduled passenger and freight services over an extensive international and domestic network, serving points in Asia, Australasia, Europe, North America and the Middle East. Domestic passenger services connect the capital, Seoul, with eleven other cities within South Korea.

For domestic and regional operations Korean Air is equipped with twelve Fokker 100s, ten McDonnell Douglas MD-82s, eight Airbus Industrie A300B4s and twenty-one A300-600/600Rs. Additional regional capacity is also provided by the long haul fleet of four Boeing 747-200Bs, three 747-300s, fifteen 747-400s and five McDonnell Douglas MD-11s. Two Boeing 747SPs are used exclusively on services to Amsterdam, Bahrain, Cairo, Jeddah, Moscow, Rome and Zurich, whilst a fleet of two A300F4s and ten 747-200Fs support Korean Air's impressive international cargo network. Korean Air has also ordered eight A330-300s, eight 777-200s and a further fifteen 747-400s, with deliveries to start between 1995 and 1997 and be completed by 1999.

The livery illustrated by Boeing 747-4B5 HL7479 was introduced in early 1984 and continues to provide Korean Air with a unique and unmistakable image. A pale shade of blue colours the entire upper fuselage and fin, below which runs an elegant silver cheatline to neatly merge with pale grey underside colouring. The tail motif, known locally as the 'Taeguk', represents the opposite forces of nature with the red and blue colouring symbolising heaven and earth respectively, and white added to promote the 'endless strength of progress'. The 'Taeguk' also forms the letter 'o' within Korean Air titles, which are displayed on the cabin roof in blue uppercase lettering.

Kenya Airways
A310-300
5Y-BFT

KLM cityhopper
PH-CHD
F28
cityhopper

KLM
PH-KCA
KLM
Royal Dutch Airlines
NO ENTRY
GATE-H

HL7479
VISIT KOREA '94
KOREAN AIR

KUWAIT AIRWAYS

Kuwait Airways was formed by private interests in March 1954 and until March 1957 was known as Kuwait National Airways. The carrier became wholly Kuwaiti Government-owned in June 1963 and today flies scheduled passenger and freight services linking the oil-rich state with major cities in Europe, the Middle and Far East, North Africa and the United States.

The carrier has now replaced aircraft that were lost or seized during the Gulf war with a combination of three Airbus Industrie A320-200s, four A310-300s and five A300-600Rs, with four A340-200s having been ordered for delivery between 1996/97. The four 747-200Bs survived the conflict and continue to be used on services to Bangkok, Bombay, Cairo, Manila and New York (via London) - although three 747-400s have been ordered to replace these aircraft with deliveries to commence in August 1995. The sole remaining 767-200 has been leased to Polynesian Airlines and will eventually be sold. Additional cargo capacity is provided by up to three Boeing 707-320Cs leased from TMA of Lebanon.

Kuwait Airways updated its livery with the introduction of new Airbus Industrie A320 aircraft from October 1992. In its revised form, illustrated by Boeing 747-269B 9K-ADD, the medium blue tail band has been expanded and is now edged with black pinstripes, with the stylised bird insignia appearing in white as before. The cheatline is arranged directly below window level in a 'straight through' manner, with its colouring and presentation based on the tail markings. Kuwait Airways titling appears in black uppercase lettering on the cabin roof, together with its Arabic equivalent, and is also promoted at the base of the fin. The livery is complimented by a white overall backdrop, and finished with a facsimile of the cheatline around the engine intakes.

LATAVIO-LATVIAN AIRLINES

Latavio was created in 1991 to assume the operations of a former Aeroflot Directorate serving the region. The carrier now provides regular scheduled international services connecting the capital, Riga, with Amsterdam, Copenhagen, Helsinki, Jonkoping, Moscow, Stockholm, Vienna and Warsaw. Domestic and regional flights are also undertaken.

The airline continues to make use of the fleet inherited from Aeroflot, which includes nine Antonov An-24s, two An-26 freighters, nine Tupolev Tu-134s and five Tu-154s. A number of Mil Mi-2 helicopters and Antonov An-2s are also used for agricultural and light utility tasks.

Tupolev Tu-134B-3 YL-LBI illustrates the full burgundy and white colouring of Latavio, which is both smart and modern by any standards. However, it should be noted that some aircraft (especially domestic types) are still being operated in basic Aeroflot markings but with substitute titles and flags. A white painted cabin exterior is in stark contrast to the rich burgundy colouring of the rear fuselage, engines and fin, and accommodates black uppercase Latavio lettering alongside a smaller Latvian Airlines inscription. The carrier's motif appears within a white enclosure and is loosely reflected by a pair of burgundy coloured fuselage bands, which are displayed on the forward cabin.

LAUDA AIR

Lauda Air was formed by Nikki Lauda in April 1979 and commenced operations as a local charter and air-taxi concern with two Fokker Friendships. Mediterranean charters were introduced in 1985 with leased BAe 1-11 equipment and two years later the carrier was licensed to begin scheduled operations. Today, charters are flown to holiday resorts in the Mediterranean, the Canary Islands, Florida, Jamaica, Mexico, St. Lucia and Santo Domingo, whilst scheduled services link Vienna with points in Australasia, Europe, the Far East and North America. The carrier is a Lufthansa partner and operates some scheduled international services via Munich. Lauda Air Italy was created in 1992 as a Milan-based subsidiary.

Three Boeing 767-300/ERs are used on scheduled routes to Bangkok, Hong Kong, Los Angeles, Melbourne, Miami, Phuket and Sydney, whilst also providing long haul charter capacity. Europe and the Mediterranean are served by a fleet of two 737-300s and two 737-400s (a third has been ordered), with three 50-seat Canadair Regional Jets used exclusively on scheduled services feeding the carrier's Vienna hub. Four Boeing 777-200/ERs have been ordered for delivery from September 1997.

Lauda Air's livery is based on a red 'L' initial, which forms an all encompassing tail motif and also heads similarly coloured Lauda titling on the cabin roof. Note: the tail motif is mirrored on the starboard side of the fuselage and therefore always points to the nose. A distinctive charcoal-coloured underside is 'cut off' in line with the fin's leading edge and trimmed with three red pinstripes (two raised and one lowered). Secondary 'Partner of Lufthansa' titles are also displayed on a white cabin roof in the same charcoal grey shade. Finally, white painted engine housings display a small angel motif above Nikki Lauda's signature, in recognition of the near fatal crash that effectively ended the Austrian racer's Formula One career.

LITHUANIAN AIRLINES

Lithuanian Airlines was formed in 1991 to succeed a former Aeroflot division and today operates scheduled international services linking the capital, Vilnius with Amsterdam, Berlin, Copenhagen, Frankfurt, London, Paris, Stockholm and Warsaw. The carrier also serves a number of regional destinations, including Ekaterinburg, Groznyg, Kiev, Mineralyne Vody, Moscow, Odessa, St. Petersburg, Samara, Tashkent and Ufa.

A single Boeing 737-200 was leased from the GPA Group in December 1991 to facilitate the expansion of the carrier's international network. This continues to be supplemented by a fleet of eight Tupolev Tu-134As and five Yakovlev Yak-42Ds, with four Antonov An-24s, three An-26s and seven Yak-42s used regionally.

The current Lithuanian Airlines livery, illustrated by Yakovlev Yak-42D LY-AAU, was introduced in the spring of 1994 to replace the interim 'LAL' image. The new design is based on a bright red underside, which flares in an upward sweep to colour the entire rear fuselage and fin, shadowed by a pale grey pinstriped cheatline. Red is also used to outline the cabin doors and emergency exits, and to colour Lithuanian Airlines titling on the cabin roof. The tail motif, which is white and set within a circular enclosure, is also reproduced underneath the forward fuselage and symbolises flight in the form of a mirrored 'L' initial. Attention is drawn to the fact that its reproduction on the fin is forward facing on both sides. The full livery, including titles, is also worn by a Lockheed JetStar of the Presidential Flight, and will eventually be adopted fleetwide.

KUWAIT AIRWAYS
الخطوط الجوية الكويتية
KUWAIT AIRWAYS
9K-ADD

LATAVIO
LATVIAN AIRLINES
YL-LBI

Lauda
Lufthansa

Lithuanian Airlines
LY-A AU
YAK-42D

LOT POLISH AIRLINES

LOT Polish Airlines was formed by the Polish Government on January 1st 1929 to take over the operations of two private companies known as Aerolot and Aero. The new national carrier went on to improve domestic services and also built up a considerable international network, reaching as far north as Helsinki and southwards to Lydda in Palestine, until the Second World War halted any future progress. Today, LOT's scheduled international network extends to Africa, Australasia, the Middle and Far East and North America, in addition to connecting Warsaw with major cities throughout Europe. Domestic services and international charters are also undertaken.

The Polish carrier is now equipped with eight ATR72s, four Boeing 737-400s, six 737-500s, two 767-200/ERs (plus one leased from Air New Zealand for the summer) and one 767-300/ER. Most former Soviet types have either been sold or grounded, although two leased Antonov An-26s remain in use with the airline to provide additional cargo capacity. LOT is planning to acquire another two Boeing 767s and has also expressed interest in the 777 for future fleet introduction.

When LOT was created in 1929 a competition was held to find an insignia for the new company. This was won by a young artist, Tadeusz Gronowski, who designed an emblem in the shape of a stylised crane in flight, enclosed in a circle. This symbol has been carried by all LOT aircraft ever since and is supported by the national flag in the current livery, illustrated by Boeing 737-45D SP-LLB. A white cabin exterior promotes high visibility LOT titling, followed by a matching midnight blue windowline which originates from around the cockpit windows. It is interesting to note that on the port (left) side of the fuselage the windowline is a continuation of the letter 'T' and underlines secondary Polish Airlines titling in black. On the opposite side, it is spaced from the letter 'L' and the secondary titling is reproduced in Polish. The engine housings mirror the forward fuselage colouring, minus the cheatline.

LUFTHANSA

Lufthansa can trace its history back to January 6th 1926 when two of Germany's leading airlines (Deutcher Aero Lloyd and Junkers Luftverkehr AG) were merged to form Deutsche Luft Hansa. D.L.H. soon established itself as one of the world's leading airlines and embarked upon many well known pioneering flights in its quest to establish a truly worldwide network. The modern day Lufthansa commenced operations on April 1st 1955 and soon set about rebuilding the pre-war network of its predecessor, which by June of that year reached across the Atlantic to New York. Today, Lufthansa's international passenger and freight network connects Germany with cities on all five continents. Subsidiary companies include Lufthansa CityLine, Lufthansa Cargo Airlines and Condor.

Airbus Industrie A310-200s, Boeing 737-200s, 747-200Bs and McDonnell Douglas DC-10-30s are gradually being phased out to make way for newer types, with many of these now stored and/or awaiting delivery to new owners. In more recent times Lufthansa has added eleven Airbus Industrie A300B4-600s, thirty-three A320-200s, twelve A310-300s, twenty A321-100s (deliveries in progress), six A340-200s, eight A340-300s (deliveries in progress), seven Boeing 737-400s, forty-six 737-300s (including eight -QCs), thirty 737-500s and seventeen 747-400s (including seven SCDs). In addition, ten Boeing 747-200Fs, one 737-300F and five McDonnell Douglas DC-8-70Fs are operated by Lufthansa Cargo Airlines.

The livery illustrated by Airbus Industrie A340-311 D-AIGD was introduced in September 1988 to succeed a similar design, which basically involved removing cheatlines and lowering the grey underside colouring to a point below wing level. It has since been adopted by Lufthansa CityLine and Lufthansa Cargo Airlines (formerly German Cargo Airlines).

LUXAIR

Luxair was formed in 1961 and until April 1962 was known as Luxembourg Airlines. Scheduled passenger services now connect the Grand Duchy of Luxembourg with Berlin, Copenhagen, Geneva, Frankfurt, Hamburg, Lisbon, London-Heathrow/Stansted, Malaga, Milan, Munich, Nice, Palma, Paris, Rome, Saarbrucken, Strasbourg and Vienna. Inclusive tour flights are also undertaken to holiday destinations in Europe and North Africa, with commuter operations the responsibility of a subsidiary trading as Luxair Commuter.

For its charter and scheduled operations Luxair is equipped with two Boeing 737-400s and two 737-500s, both of which are configured in a single class, all-economy layout. The larger -400 series aircraft are mostly used on scheduled routes to Malaga and Palma and charters throughout the Mediterranean region. Four turboprop Fokker 50s are used on 'thinner' regional routes, supplemented by three 29-seat Embraer EMB-120ER Brasilias operated by Luxair's commuter affiliate.

The livery illustrated by Boeing 757-4C9 LX-LGF colours the Boeing 737 and Fokker 50 aircraft, whilst the Brasilias have adopted a separate Luxair Commuter image. When representing the national carrier, the design features an aqua-coloured cheatline arrangement and a matching tail backdrop. Luxair titles are displayed in black upper case lettering on the cabin roof, alongside the flags of Luxembourg and the European Community. The tail motif appears in the form of an L-shaped arrow and is reproduced in white within a spherical enclosure. The cabin exterior is painted white down to wing level and grey thereafter, and completes a design that could be said does little to promote the modern types operated.

MAERSK AIR

Maersk Air was formed in 1969 and commenced operations in January 1970 as a Copenhagen-based charter carrier. The airline has since developed a scheduled network which connects Billund with Amsterdam, Brussels, Copenhagen, Frankfurt, London-Gatwick and Stockholm; and Copenhagen with Bornholm, the Faroe Islands, London-Gatwick, Odense and Vojens. Inclusive-tour charters continue to be undertaken from the Nordic countries to holiday destinations in Europe. Maersk Air also plays an active role in the aircraft leasing market.

The airline is equipped with a fleet of nine Fokker 50s, thirteen Boeing 737-300s (plus four on order) and four 737-400s. Maersk Air has also ordered six 737-700s, with deliveries to begin in the latter part of 1997. Most scheduled routes are served by the turboprop Fokker 50s, with the Boeing twin jets operating major trunk routes between Copenhagen and Billund, and to London and the Faroe Islands. Up to ten 737-300s are leased out at any one time.

The livery illustrated by Boeing 737-3L9 OY-MML has coloured Maersk Air's fleet for over twenty years, having been introduced in its original form by the carrier's first Boeing 720s in early 1973. Pale blue fuselage and fin colouring is complimented by a dual coloured cheatline of medium and dark blue, which is placed below window level and trimmed either side in white, as are the passenger doors. The tail motif is in the form of a seven pointed star and appears neatly 'boxed' within a white outlined enclosure. The motif is also reproduced on the forward cabin roof alongside Maersk titles in white uppercase lettering. Note: the blue tint is always added to the motif when reproduced over a grey or white backdrop (see engine housings), which sometimes applies to aircraft that are leased in for relatively short periods.

POLISH AIRLINES
LOT
SP-LLB

Sheraton
Lufthansa
D-AIGD

LUXAIR

MAERSK
OY-MML

MALAYSIA AIRLINES

Malaysia Airlines was formed by the Malaysian Government in April 1971 to succeed Malaysia-Singapore Airlines (MSA), which had been formed as a joint venture between the two countries five years earlier. Services began on October 1st 1972 and now connect Kuala Lumpur with cities throughout the Asia-Pacific region, Europe, the Middle and Far East and North America. An extensive domestic network is also maintained.

The carrier's short to medium requirement is met by eleven Fokker 50s and seven DHC-6 Twin Otter 300s (for domestic operations), two Boeing 737-300F freighters, forty-six 737-400s, nine 737-500s and four Airbus Industrie A300B4s. For long haul and high density routes Malaysia Airlines is equipped with a fleet of two Boeing 747-200Bs, one 747-300, eleven 747-400s (plus two on order) and six McDonnell Douglas DC-10-30s. Ten Airbus Industrie A330-300s have also been ordered for delivery between 1994 and 1996.

The livery illustrated by Boeing 747-4H6 9M-MHM was introduced in 1987 to replace the previous red and white Malaysian Airline System image. In its revised form, a combination of red and blue has been used to colour the cheatlines, which start at the nose as a narrow windowline and eventually flare under the lower rear fuselage. The same combination colours the new corporate motif, which is based on the Kalantan Kite of old but reproduced larger than before and over a white coloured backdrop. Malaysia titles are predominantly blue in colour, with the letters m, a and s featuring subtle red highlights in recognition of the full Malaysian Airline System name. Positioned on the cabin roof, the titles appear in a unique corporate typeface and are preceded by the national flag. The lower fuselage and engine housings are finished in a solid grey shade, in preference to white.

MALEV HUNGARIAN AIRLINES

Malev was formed in April 1946 as a joint Hungarian-Soviet venture and until November 1954 was known as Maszovlet. Now a public limited company, Malev operates a network of scheduled passenger and cargo services to points in Europe, the Middle East, North Africa and North America.

The current fleet includes six Tupolev Tu-134A-3s, twelve Tu-154B-2s (one operated as a freighter), four Boeing 737-200s, four 737-300s, two 767-200/ERs and two Yakovlev Yak-40s. The carrier is planning to phase out all Russian-built equipment by the end of 1995 and there is talk of Alitalia, which has a financial interest in Malev, transferring some of its surplus McDonnell Douglas DC-9-30s to the airline. Another possibility is that Malev will order four Fokker 70s to replace its 68-seat Tu-134As.

The latest Malev livery, illustrated by Boeing 737-3Y0 HA-LEG, features a stylish portrayal of the Hungarian flag over a solid blue backdrop, which is lowered in line with the fin's leading edge to colour the entire rear fuselage section. Malev titles are similarly coloured and appear on the cabin roof in a unique corporate typeface, alongside secondary Hungarian Airlines wording in black. The design is balanced by a blue painted nose radome, which adds colour and distinction to an otherwise white painted fuselage.

MANX AIRLINES

Manx Airlines was originally formed as a joint venture between British Midland Airways and Air UK and initiated services between the Isle of Man and London-Heathrow on November 1st 1982. Now a member of the Airlines of Britain Group, Manx Airlines is one of Europe's largest regional airlines with a comprehensive domestic route structure radiating from hubs at Cardiff, Liverpool, Ronaldsway (Isle of Man) and Southampton. The carrier also operates internationally to Brussels and Paris.

A modern and well-equipped commuter fleet currently includes fourteen British Aerospace ATPs and ten Jetstream 41s, with three BAe 146s providing additional capacity on domestic trunk routes.

The focal point of the current Manx Airlines livery is provided by a representation of the Isle's national symbol, which is reproduced in the form of a red and white tail band and set against a green coloured backdrop. Illustrated by British Aerospace 146-200 G-MIMA, the design also features a delicate cheatline arrangement, which appears below window level in two values of green, with the more prominent shade underscoring lighter pinstripes and accommodating secondary 'Skianyn Vannin' (Manx Airlines) titling in white. Gaelic also influences the style of lowercase Manx lettering, which is displayed on the cabin roof in green and above the tail motif in white.

MARTINAIR

Martinair was formed on May 24th 1958 and initially undertook executive charters, aerial advertising and sightseeing flights under the name of Martins Air Charter. By the summer of 1964 the company had absorbed two smaller Dutch operators and was 25% owned by KLM. Passenger and freight charters began to be developed on a worldwide scale and in April 1968 the company's name was changed to Martinair Holland. Today, the carrier operates scheduled passenger flights connecting Amsterdam with points in the Caribbean, Mexico and the United States, as well as inclusive-tour charters to holiday destinations in the Mediterranean and Canary Islands, and to Phuket in Thailand. Regular cargo services are operated to points in North and South America, the Middle and Far East and Australia.

A modern all-jet fleet currently includes one Airbus Industrie A310-200C, five Boeing 767-300/ERs, two 747-200B, one 747-200F freighter and three McDonnell Douglas DC-10-30CFs (to be replaced by four MD-11CFs during 1995). The carrier will add a sixth 767-300/ER (leased from ILFC) and a McDonnell Douglas MD-11F freighter to its fleet in November 1995.

The livery illustrated by Boeing 767-31A/ER PH-MCG was introduced in its original form in 1974 and does little to emphasise the modern widebodied fleet now operated by the carrier. A red windowline starts at the nose and continues in a conventional 'straight through' manner, stopping short of the horizontal stabilisers at the rear. The tail motif is similarly coloured and appears in the form of a stylised 'M' initial, with the leading stroke sweeping back on itself (having once been an extension of the cheatline). Martinair titles are displayed in black uppercase lettering, with the fuselage painted white to wing level and left natural metal below.

Visit Malaysia Year 1990
malaysia

MALEV Hungarian Airlines
HA-LEG

manx
manx
G-MIMA

Martinair

MEA-MIDDLE EAST AIRLINES

The national carrier of the Lebanon, MEA was formed in May 1945 by a group of local businessmen and initiated service between Beirut and Nicosia in November of that year. The company continued to expand its international network, aided by a merger with Air Liban in November 1965 and the acquisition of Lebanese International Airlines' traffic rights in 1969. Destinations currently served from Beirut include Abidjan, Abu Dhabi, Accra, Aden, Amman, Athens, Bahrain, Berlin, Brussels, Cairo, Colombo, Copenhagen, Damascus, Dhahran, Doha, Dubai, Frankfurt, Freetown, Geneva, Istanbul, Jeddah, Kano, Kuwait, Khartoum, Lagos, Larnaca, London, Madrid, Milan, Nice, Paris, Riyadh, Rome, Singapore, Sydney, Tunis and Zurich.

Years of internal conflict have prevented MEA from developing at a similar pace to other carriers in the region, and it is therefore not surprising to find no less than eight Boeing 707s still operating regular scheduled passenger services for the airline. Three Boeing 747-200Bs that were originally delivered in 1975 are now also flying for MEA after spending many years in exile, and have been joined by two Airbus Industrie A310-200s (leased from KLM) and two A310-300s (leased from Polaris).

Inspiration for the MEA livery was obtained from the national flag, which lends not only the red and white colouring but also the Cedar of Lebanon motif - this having deep religious significance in the region. In its latest form, illustrated by Boeing 747-2B4B N202AE, a narrow red cheatline starts at the nose and is then broken to accommodate bold MEA initials, before continuing below window level to the rear. The application of the tail motif remains much the same as before, with a raised red backdrop underscored by a facsimile of the cheatline.

MERIDIANA

Meridiana was formed as Alisarda in March 1963 and began life as a charter and air-taxi operator. Scheduled services were introduced from May 1966 and now connect numerous domestic and European cities from Bologna, Catania, Florence, Olbia (Sardinia), Cagliari, Rome and Verona. The carrier's international network serves Barcelona, Frankfurt, Geneva, London-Gatwick, Munich, Nice, Paris and Zurich. The current name was adopted in September 1991 to align with Meridiana of Spain, a sister company that later ceased operations in 1992.

A modern all-jet fleet consists of eight McDonnell Douglas MD-82s, six DC-9-50s and four BAe 146-200s.

Meridiana's livery, illustrated by British Aerospace 146-200 I-FLRW, is based on the previous Alisarda image. A red and blue cheatline arrangement, dissected by a yellow pinstripe, starts at the nose and continues at window level, neatly separating the fuselage colours of white and grey. The cheatline is repeated at the base of the tail, where the red expands to penetrate a white spherical motif in forming a series of outlined peaks. Meridiana titles are displayed on the forward cabin roof in black lettering, with the Italian flag appearing alongside the registration letters at the rear. The corporate motif is also promoted on the engine housings, only this time in red on white.

MONARCH AIRLINES

Monarch Airlines was formed in June 1967 and commenced charter operations from Luton airport the following April with a fleet of Bristol Britannias. Today, inclusive-tour charter flights are also flown from Gatwick, Stansted and Manchester to holiday resorts in Africa, the Caribbean, Europe, the Asia-Pacific region and the United States. The 'seat only' market to Spain and the Canary Islands is served by scheduled year-round flights connecting Luton with Alicante, Malaga, Menorca and Tenerife.

The carrier's fleet is based on some of the latest types offered by Airbus Industrie and Boeing, including seven 179-seat A320-200s, eight 757-200s and four 361-seat A300-600Rs.

The livery illustrated by Airbus Industrie A300B4-605R G-MAJS was introduced with the delivery of the company's first Boeing 757 in March 1983 and continued the Monarch tradition of using yellow and black to colour its fleet. This highly effective combination now appears in the form of a bold 'straight through' windowline, underlining black Monarch titling on the forward cabin roof. Black is also used to colour the corporate motif, a crowned 'M' initial, which is displayed at the centre of a white painted tail, with the fuselage painted white down to wing level and grey thereafter.

NIGERIA AIRWAYS

Nigeria Airways was formed in 1958 to succeed West African Airways, which had been created twelve years earlier as a subsidiary of BOAC. Today, the carrier provides extensive domestic services connecting all nineteen states in the Nigerian Federation with key cities throughout the country. International services connect the capital, Lagos, with points in East and West Africa, Europe, the Middle East and North America, with additional flights also provided from Kano and Port Harcourt.

The airline is currently thought to be operating a fleet of six Boeing 737-200s, two Airbus Industrie A310-200s and two McDonnell Douglas DC-10-30s. Another two 737-200s and two A310-200s are currently parked, as are three Boeing 707-320Cs, but could be returned to service in the near future as the carrier begins to emerge from a long period of cut backs and depression. Another two DC-10-30s could also be added for proposed expansion.

The livery illustrated by McDonnell Douglas DC-10-30 5N-ANN was originally designed as part of a Federal Government proposal to privatise the carrier's international operations under the name of Air Nigeria. This is still likely to happen at some time in the future, but in the meantime all operations are being conducted under the Nigeria Airways banner. The new Air Nigeria livery has been adopted by DC-10 and A310 aircraft and features a gold and white coloured eagle motif as its centrepiece. The design is based on a wedged cheatline of gold, dark and mid-green, which breaks formation at the rear to colour the tail and lower fuselage. Titles, currently reading Nigeria Airways, are displayed in a lowercase style on the cabin roof and fin, in green and white respectively, and appear close to the eagle in both cases. A white painted cabin exterior provides the perfect backdrop for the livery, and extends to the engine housings where yet another 'golden' eagle is accommodated.

MEA
N202AE

Meridiana
I-FLRW

Monarch
G-MAJS
A300-600R

nigeria airways
nigeria airways
5N-ANN

NORTHWEST AIRLINES

Northwest Airlines can trace its history back to August 1926 when it was formed under the name of Northwest Airways to carry mail between Chicago and St. Paul under a U.S. Post Office contract. The airline was renamed Northwest Orient in 1934 and in the years that followed a vast domestic and trans-Pacific passenger and freight network was established. Known as Northwest Airlines since 1985, the carrier now provides scheduled passenger services to points in Canada, the Caribbean, Europe, Mexico and the Asia-Pacific region, with major domestic traffic hubs located at Detroit, Minneapolis/St. Paul and Memphis.

A large fleet includes twenty-two McDonnell Douglas DC-9-10s, ninety-one DC-9-30s, twelve DC-9-40s (ex-SAS), twenty-eight DC-9-50s, eight MD-80s, fifty Airbus Industrie A320-200s, fifty-six Boeing 727-200s, thirty-three 757-200s, twenty-one McDonnell Douglas DC-10-40s, eight DC-10-30s (ex-Swissair), twelve Boeing 747-100s (the majority now stored), twenty 747-200Bs, seven 747-200F freighters and ten 747-400s. On order: forty 757-200s (delivery between 1995 and 1998), four 747-400s and sixteen A330-300s (delivery between 1996 and 1997). Seventy-nine DC-9s are also being upgraded and refurbished under an intensive life extension programme.

The livery illustrated by Boeing 747-451 N662US was introduced in June 1989.to welcome the new Airbus Industrie A320s to the fleet. The design is based on all-encompassing fuselage bands of red, grey and white, with the more prominent grey shade accommodating Northwest titling in white uppercase lettering. The lower bands are separated by a smart mid-blue cheatline, which starts as a tapered pinstripe and becomes progressively wider at the rear, with the upper red colouring bleeding onto the tail. The tail motif graphically portrays Northwest in the form of a letter 'N' and west facing compass point, both enclosed within a white outlined globe.

OLYMPIC AIRWAYS

Olympic Airways was formed in April 1957 when Aristotle Onassis acquired the Government-owned TAE Greek National Airlines, which had itself been created six years earlier through the merger of three pioneering Greek airlines. Ownership reverted to the Government in August 1975 and for a while operations were suspended. Today, the carrier's network connects Athens with points in Africa, Asia, Australia, Europe, the Middle and Far East and North America. Local operations are supplemented by the domestic and inter-island network of Olympic Aviation, which is a wholly-owned subsidiary.

A fleet standardised on Airbus Industrie and Boeing types currently includes eleven 737-200s, seven 737-400s, eight A300B4s, four A300-600Rs and four 747-200Bs. Proposed cutbacks will reportedly lead to the sale of two Boeing 747s and the return of two leased A300B4s, with the 727-200 fleet having already been grounded at Athens.

It is currently possible to see Olympic aircraft wearing three different liveries, with the design illustrated by 747-212B SX-OAD having been introduced in April 1994 to succeed a more colourful, yet relatively short lived image. The design previous to that is also still worn by some members of the fleet. In its latest form the livery uses a medium shade of blue to colour a trimmed cheatline and fin, which are brought together by the upward expansion of a narrow pinstripe. The Olympic rings have provided the focal point of all past and present Olympic liveries and continue to be displayed in their traditional colours on the fin. Olympic titles appear in the usual corporate style and are preceded by 'fluttering' EC and Greek pendants, with the cabin painted white down to door level and grey thereafter.

ONUR AIR

Onur Air is an Istanbul-based charter airline that commenced operations in the summer of 1992 with two leased Airbus Industrie A320s. The carrier now flies to points in Austria, Belgium, Finland, France, Germany, Holland, Israel, Switzerland and the United Kingdom.

Five Airbus Industrie A320-200s currently equip the fleet, although additional aircraft are often leased in to provide additional capacity during the peak summer months (July to October).

Onur Air's livery, illustrated by Airbus Industrie A320-231 TC-ONB, is based on delicate lines of red and blue over a white exterior finish. A simple cheatline starts at the nose and continues in a conventional 'straight through' manner, below the window level, to the rear. The red and blue theme is also used to colour a partly encircled tail motif, with blue Onur Air titling preceded by the Turkish flag on the cabin roof.

PALAIR MACEDONIAN

Palair Macedonian was created in the newly formed Republic of Macedonia in 1992 and commenced operations using a small fleet of Antonov An-24s and Tupolev Tu-154s leased from Balkan Bulgarian Airlines. A subsidiary of the Palastourist Group, a travel and tourist organisation, the carrier now provides scheduled services connecting Skopje with destinations in Belgium, Germany, Holland, Russia, Slovenia, Switzerland and Turkey.

The Antonov An-24s have since returned to Balkan and been replaced by two Fokker F.28 Fellowships, leased from TAT European Airlines. The carrier's association with the Dutch manufacturer was later strengthened with the signing of a contract for two Fokker 100s to replace leased Tu-154s during the winter '93/94 season.

The livery illustrated by Fokker 100 F-OLGA was first applied to a Fokker Fellowship and has since been adopted fleetwide. In its original form the design featured white overall fuselage colouring with red titles, but perhaps this was simply a quick and cost effective way of repainting aircraft for relatively short lease contracts.

NORTHWEST

OLYMPIC
SX-OAD

ONUR AIR
TC-ONB

Palair Macedonian
F-OLGA

PHILIPPINE AIRLINES

Philippine Airlines was created by private interests in February 1941 and commenced operations on a domestic basis on March 15th of that year, only to be interrupted by the outbreak of war in the Pacific a few months later. Services recommenced on February 14th 1946 and were soon expanded to points beyond the Philippine archipelago. Ownership later passed to the Philippine Government, although in 1992 a 67% controlling interest was sold to a consortium of local banking investors. Today, Philippine Airlines flies internationally to Abu Dhabi, Bandar Seri Begawan, Bangkok, Brisbane, Dhahran, Dubai, Frankfurt, Fukuoka, Ho Chi Minh City, Hong Kong, Honolulu, Jakarta, Jeddah, Kaohsiung, Kota Kinabalu, Kuala Lumpur, London, Los Angeles, Melbourne, New York, Paris, Riyadh, Rome, San Francisco, Seoul, Singapore, Sydney, Taipei and Tokyo. An extensive domestic and regional network is also maintained.

A large fleet includes ten Fokker 50s, twelve Boeing 737-300s and eight Airbus Industrie A300B4s for domestic and regional operations, with longer sectors operated by eleven Boeing 747-200Bs (including two leased from Singapore Airlines) and two 747-400s (two more on order for delivery in 1995).

The livery illustrated by Boeing 747-2F6B N742PR was introduced in late 1986 and features a colourful representation of the national flag as its centrepiece. A bright sun burst emanates from interlocking triangles of red and blue, with its penetrating rays arranged in honour of the first eight provinces to revolt against Spain during the independence movement of 1898. A white cabin exterior plays host to blue Philippines titling, with a small national flag reproduced in its correct (horizontal) form below the tail motif.

PIA-PAKISTAN INTERNATIONAL AIRWAYS

The state-owned airline of Pakistan was formed in 1954 to link East Pakistan with West Pakistan (now Bangladesh), using Lockheed Super Constellations. International scheduled passenger and freight services commenced in 1955, to Cairo and London, and now connect Pakistan with points in Africa, Asia, Europe, the Middle and Far East, and North America. In addition, an extensive domestic network is also maintained.

Mainstay of the domestic fleet is the Fokker Friendship, of which fourteen are employed on services connecting the capital Karachi with no less than twenty points within Pakistan. A single international Friendship service also connects Gwadar with Muscat (Oman). Two DHC-6 Twin Otter 300s are used locally between Islamabad, Muzaffarabad, Rawala Kot and Peshawar. Additional domestic and regional capacity is provided by six Boeing 737-300s, nine Airbus Industrie A300B4s and six A310-300s, with Boeing 747-200Bs also used on the busy trunk routes connecting Karachi, Lahore and Islamabad. The Airbus A300B4s and A310-300s operate mostly to points in Africa, Asia and the Middle East, with the latter type also serving Athens, Copenhagen, London, Paris, Rome and Zurich in Europe, as well as Toronto in Canada. All other long haul or high density services are the responsibility of eight Boeing 747-200s, which in addition to supplementing the Airbus fleet regionally also fly to Amsterdam, Frankfurt, Istanbul, London, Manchester, Moscow, Paris, New York and Toronto.

Inspiration for the PIA livery, illustrated by Airbus Industrie A310-308 AP-BEU (F-WWCD), is provided by the green and white colouring of the national flag, which combines to form the PIA tail motif and also to colour the fuselage. Bright diagonal bands of blue and green have now been added to shortened underside colouring, preceded by a representation of PIA initials in Urdu. The remainder of the cabin is painted white, with green Pakistan titling displayed above window level.

PREMIAIR

Premiair was created on January 1st 1994 following a merger between two of Scandinavia's leading holiday charter airlines, namely Scanair (owned by SAS Leisure) and Conair of Denmark (owned by the Spies Group). Inclusive tour charters are flown from points throughout Scandinavia to holiday destinations in Africa, Europe, the Far East, Mexico, the Caribbean and North America. SAS Leisure's interest in the company has since been sold to Airtours of the United Kingdom.

The carrier is equipped with six Airbus Industrie A320-200s and four McDonnell Douglas DC-10-10s. One of the three ex-Conair A300B4-120s has also been retained to operate a programme of charters from Billund in Denmark, with the other two having been leased to a Conair subsidiary operating from Germany.

Premiair's livery, illustrated by McDonnell Douglas DC-10-10 SE-DHC, effectively merges the colours of Scanair (orange) and Conair (blue) into a design that has all the features of a typical holiday airline. Whether or not the eclipse on the fin was always meant to represent a short lived partnership is perhaps coincidental, but SAS Leisure's interest in Premiair was certainly just that. A white cabin exterior promotes black Premiair titling, which is also repeated on the engine housings, with the first letter 'i' dotted in orange and the second in blue.

QANTAS

The oldest airline in the English speaking world, Qantas was originally formed in November 1920 as Queensland and Northern Territory Aerial Services. International services were introduced in 1934 and by 1947 Qantas had inaugurated its 'Kangaroo' route to London. Today, the carrier provides scheduled international services connecting Australia with Europe, the Middle and Far East, Africa, Asia and North America. The domestic network of Australian Airlines was absorbed on September 14th 1992 as part of the Government's privatisation policy. Australia Asia Airways is a wholly-owned subsidiary which offers scheduled passenger and freight services connecting Sydney and Brisbane with Taipei.

Including the fleet inherited from Australian Airlines, Qantas is now equipped with sixteen Boeing 737-300s, seventeen 737-400s, five 747-200Bs, six 747-300s, eighteen 747-400s, seven 767-200/ERs, fifteen 767-300/ERs and four Airbus Industrie A300B4s. In addition, two Boeing 747SPs are operated by its Australia Asia Airways subsidiary.

The livery illustrated by Boeing 747-438 VH-OJO was introduced in June 1985 and now colours all members of the fleet, including the domestic 737s and A300B4s inherited from Australian Airlines. Created by the Lunn Design Group of Sydney, its focal point is a winged Kangaroo motif, which is displayed in white over an extension of red tail colouring - the leading edge of which is trimmed in gold. A white cabin exterior accommodates Qantas titling in black uppercase lettering, supported by secondary 'The Spirit of Australia' wording below. The red and gold tail colouring is reproduced on the winglets of the 747-400s, with the corporate motif promoted on the white painted engine housings of all types operated.

Philippines

PIA
Pakistan
A310

premiair

QANTAS
LONGREACH
THE SPIRIT OF AUSTRALIA

ROYAL AIRLINES

Quebec based Royal Airlines was formed in 1991 and commenced domestic and regional charter operations the following year with a former Dan Air Boeing 727-200. The collapse of other charter carriers (including Worldways and later Nationair) provided opportunities for expansion and by the summer of 1993 Royal Airlines was crossing the Atlantic to points in the United Kingdom and mainland Europe. Today, charters are flown from several Canadian cities to holiday destinations in Europe, Mexico, the United States and the Caribbean, including Aruba, Barbados, Brussels, Cancun, Fort Lauderdale, Freeport, Las Vegas, London-Gatwick, Manzanillo, Montego Bay, Nassau, Paris, Porlamar, Puerto Plata, Puerto Vallarta, St. Maarten, St. Petersburg and Varadero Beach.

The carrier is currently equipped with a fleet of seven Boeing 727-200s and two ex-Air Canada Lockheed TriStar-100s.

The livery adopted by Royal Airlines is every much as regal as the bold 'Royal' titling on the forward fuselage may suggest. Illustrated by Lockheed TriStar-100 C-FTNI, the design uses a combination of deep blue and gold in the form of a veil covering the entire rear fuselage and fin. This provides the setting for a gold coloured wreath, which is something placed on the head as a sign of honour and also has many regal qualities. The titles are applied in a matching shade of blue over a white cabin exterior, with the Canadian flag displayed on the raised engine of both types currently operated.

ROYAL AIR MAROC

Royal Air Maroc was formed through the merger of Societe Air Atlas and Air Maroc in June 1953 and was known until 1957 as Compagnie Cherifienne de Transports Aeriens-CGTA. Today, scheduled international flights serve points in Africa, Europe, the Middle East and North America, with a domestic and regional network linking the capital, Casablanca, with Agadir, Al Hoceima, Dakhla, Fez, Goulimime, Laayoune, Marrakech, Ouarzazate, Oujda, Rabat, Tangier, Tan Tan, Tetuan and Gran Canaria.

The airline currently operates a fleet of two ATR42-300s, two Boeing 707-320Cs, six 727-200s, three 737-200s, two 737-200Cs, six 737-400s, two 757-200s, one 747SP, one 747-200 and one 747-400. The larger Boeing 747s operate long haul routes to Montreal and New York and also provide additional capacity on trunk routes to Cairo, Geneva, Jeddah and Rome. A further twelve Boeing 737s are being acquired to replace 727-200s and 737-200s.

The current Royal Air Maroc livery, illustrated by Boeing 747SP-44 CN-RMS, uses the flag colours of red and green to colour a simple 'straight through' cheatline arrangement, which is divided by a white pinstripe and tapered at both ends. On the Boeing 747s (all models) it appears as a bold windowline, whereas on the narrowbodied types the cheatline is arranged below window level and is less profound. Royal Air Maroc titles are displayed in red lowercase lettering on the starboard (right) cabin roof, with their Arabic equivalent appearing on the opposite side. The tail motif is also inspired by the national flag and features red RAM initials surmounted by a green and red shooting star. Grey is used to colour the undersides and engine housings of most types operated, although on the 757s the lower fuselage is left in a natural metal finish, with the original 'winged star' corporate motif discreetly displayed on the engines of all fleet members.

ROYAL BRUNEI AIRLINES

The tiny oil-rich state of Brunei, in southeast Asia, is linked with the outside world via scheduled passenger services flown by the government-owned national flag carrier, Royal Brunei Airlines. Formed on November 18th 1974, the airline initially operated Boeing 737-200s over a regional network, but today links the capital, Bandar Seri Begawan, with points reaching as far as Europe and Australasia.

Regional operations are now conducted with a reduced fleet of two Boeing 757s, with a third aircraft having been leased to Myanmar International Airlines. In addition to serving Bangkok, Bombay, Darwin, Denpasar-Bali, Hong Kong, Kota Kinabalu and Kuching (Malaysia) and Taipei, the '757s also supplement wide bodied 767-300/ERs on major trunk routes to Bangkok, Jakarta, Manila and Singapore. Routes to Abu Dhabi, Bahrain, Beijing, Cairo, Dubai, Frankfurt, Jeddah, Kuala Lumpur, London, Perth and Zurich are exclusive to a rapidly expanding fleet of 767-300/ERs, which provide increased capacity and range for future route expansion.

The current livery, illustrated by Boeing 767-33A/ER V8-RBF, was adopted in early 1986 to coincide with the May delivery of Royal Brunei's first Boeing 757. Based on the Brunei flag, as was the previous design, the livery features a bright yellow-painted lower cabin, which is guided onto the fin by a series of yellow and black pinstripes to compliment the national symbol. The Sultan of Brunei's personal VIP fleet, which includes Boeing 727-200 and Airbus Industrie A340-200 equipment, also promotes the livery of the national carrier.

ROYAL JORDANIAN AIRLINES

Royal Jordanian Airlines was created in December 1963 to succeed Jordan Airways, which had been formed only two years earlier. Known until December 1986 as Alia, the carrier now provides scheduled international passenger and freight services connecting the capital, Amman, with Abu Dhabi, Aden, Amsterdam, Ankara, Athens, Bahrain, Bangkok, Beirut, Berlin, Brussels, Cairo, Calcutta, Casablanca, Chicago, Colombo, Delhi, Dhahran, Doha, Dubai, Frankfurt, Geneva, Istanbul, Jakarta, Jeddah, Karachi, Kuala Lumpur, Larnaca, London, Madrid, Montreal, Muscat, New York, Paris, Riyadh, Rome, Singapore, Toronto, Tunis and Vienna. The city of Aqaba is also served domestically.

The airline is equipped with two Airbus Industrie A320-200s, four A310-300s, two Boeing 727-200s and five Lockheed TriStar-500s, with additional cargo capacity provided by three Boeing 707-320C freighters. Royal Jordanian plans to add five A340-300s between 1995 and 2000 (to replace TriStar-500s) and three additional A320-200s (to replace 727-200s), at which point the fleet will be standardised on Airbus Industrie equipment.

The livery illustrated by Airbus Industrie A310-304 F-ODVH was introduced in December 1986 to replace the former Alia image. Created by Walter Landor Associates, it uses charcoal grey to colour the upper fuselage and fin, with finer details added in shades of gold, red and black, and the lower cabin painted white. The windows are underscored by a narrow red pinstripe, above a more solid band of gold, and like the passenger exits are outlined in white. Gold is also used to colour Royal Jordanian titles, in English and Arabic, and the Hashemite Crown motif on the tail. Tapered black stripes emanate from the fin's trailing edge, with red trimming the highest point in the interests of visibility and safety.

ROYAL

الخطوط الملكية المغربية
CN-RMS
RAM

ROYAL BRUNEI

F-ODVH
ROYAL JORDANIAN
Esso

ROYAL NEPAL AIRLINES

Royal Nepal Airlines was formed by the Government of Nepal on July 1st 1958 to take over all domestic routes as well as international services between Nepal and India. The carrier continues to provide domestic links throughout the country, but has since expanded its international network to connect Kathmandu with Bangkok, Bombay, Calcutta, Delhi, Dubai, Frankfurt, Hong Kong, London-Gatwick, Paris and Singapore.

A modern international fleet includes two Boeing 757-200s and a leased Airbus Industrie A310-300, with domestic operations conducted by nine DHC-6 Twin Otter 300s, two British Aerospace 748s and a five-seater Pilatus Turbo Porter.

The airline's current livery, illustrated by Boeing 757-2F8 9N-ACA, is based on diagonal bands of red and blue, which rise from the lower rear fuselage to colour the tail. Blue Royal Nepal Airlines titling is reproduced in English on the port (left) side and Sanskrit on the starboard, in both cases preceded by the national flag, with the traditional 'winged Budha' symbol displayed beneath the cockpit windows. A white cabin exterior is extended to the engine housings, where on the Boeing 757s the national colours of red and blue are repeated in similar fashion to the tail.

SABENA - BELGIAN WORLD AIRLINES

Sabena was formed on May 23rd 1923 to succeed Syndicat National pour l'Etide de Transports Aeriens (SNETA), which had been established three years earlier to create air routes to neighbouring European countries, as well as a separate network within the Belgian Congo. By 1938 Sabena's European routes penetrated Germany, the Netherlands, Scandinavia, France, Czechoslovakia, Austria and the United Kingdom, and there was also a weekly Belgium-Congo service. Today, the Belgian national carrier provides scheduled international services connecting Brussels with points in Africa, Asia, Europe, the Middle and Far East and North America. Subsidiary companies include Delta Air Transport and Sobelair. Sabena is also associated with Air France.

The carrier is equipped with a fleet of three Airbus Industrie A310-300s, nine Boeing 737-200s, four 737-200Cs, six 737-300s, three 737-400s, six 737-500s, one 747-200B (leased from Air France), two 747-300s and three McDonnell Douglas DC-10-30CFs (including one leased from Lufthansa), with four new Airbus Industrie A340-200s having been leased to Air France since delivery. Regional capacity is provided by ten Embraer Brasilias, three Fokker F.28 Fellowships, six British Aerospace 146-200s and one 146-300 (operated by Delta Air Transport) and five Dash 8-300s (operated by Schreiner Airways).

Sabena's latest livery, illustrated by Boeing 747-228B F-GCBB, was created in the image of Air France to facilitate the interchange of aircraft between the two fleets. The livery, although based on the white exterior colouring of Air France, has been taken a step further in featuring secondary fuselage titling in a pale blue tint. A similar livery has been adopted by subsidiaries Sobelair (see) and Delta Air Transport.

SAS - SCANDINAVIAN AIRLINES SYSTEM

SAS was originally formed as OSAS on August 1st 1946 to operate the overseas services of the national airlines of Sweden, Norway and Denmark, namely SILA (Svensk Intercontinental Lufttraffik), DNL (Det Norske Luftfartselskap) and DDL (Det Danske Liftfartselskap), with the assets, aircraft and operations being divided in the ratio 3-2-2 respectively. The first flight under SAS auspices was undertaken on August 5th 1946 by a DNL Douglas DC-4. Today, services connect the Scandinavian capitals of Copenhagen, Oslo and Stockholm with points in Africa, Asia, the Middle and Far East and North and South America. An extensive domestic, regional and European network is also maintained, with Linjeflyg having been absorbed in 1992.

For domestic and regional operations SAS is equipped with a fleet of twenty-two Fokker 50s (op. by Scandinavian Commuter) and nineteen Fokker F.28 Fellowships (ex-Linjeflyg). These are supplemented by a large McDonnell Douglas DC-9/MD-80 fleet, which includes nine DC-9-20s, twenty-six DC-9-40s, thirty-one MD-81s, sixteen MD-82s, two MD-83s and sixteen MD-87s. Additional range and capacity is provided by fourteen Boeing 767-300/ERs. A fleet of twelve Boeing 737-500s (ex-Linjeflyg) is slowly being transferred/leased to British Midland - in which SAS has a financial interest. SAS has also ordered six MD-90-30s for delivery between May and August 1996.

A sleek Scandinavian image is enhanced by diagonal fuselage bands in the national colours of Denmark, Norway and Sweden respectively, set against a white cabin exterior. Scandinavian titling is reproduced in dark blue, edged in gold, in the same style and colour as SAS initials displayed on the fin. The national flags of the three participating nations appear in the same order as the fuselage rhombus, on the engine housings of the McDonnell Douglas and Fokker twinjets and the upper rear fuselage of types with wing-mounted engines. The livery was designed by Walter Landor Associates and introduced in 1983.

SAUDIA - SAUDI ARABIAN AIRLINES

Saudia was formed in 1945 by the Saudi Arabian Government and commenced local operations in 1947 with three Douglas DC-3s. Today, international services are operated from Dhahran, Jeddah and Riyadh and serve points in Africa, Asia, the Middle and Far East and North America.

The airline is currently equipped with eleven Airbus Industrie A300-600s, seventeen Boeing 737-200s, two 737-200Cs, eight 747-100Bs, one 747SP, ten 747-300s and seventeen Lockheed TriStar-200s. Up to five 747-100s and three 747-200F freighters are also leased. The carrier is about to embark on a major fleet renewal programme, with an order for over fifty aircraft expected to include twenty-nine Boeing 737s (CFM powered), five 747-400s, twelve 777s and fifteen McDonnell Douglas MD-11s. Saudia is expected to convert some of its TriStar aircraft into freighters as the new fleet is phased in.

The current Saudia livery, illustrated by Boeing 747-368 HZ-AIM, has now served the airline for many years and will no doubt be changed before any fleet modernisation takes place. A sub-divided cheatline arrangement in two values of green above two values of blue, separated by a white pinstripe, provides a base for white upper colouring on which black Saudia and secondary Saudi Arabian Airlines titling is displayed. The titles are preceded by the national flag and arranged in English and Arabic, with each language given a supporting role. The tail motif, consisting of two swords crossed before a palm tree, is based on the state arms and reproduced on a white inverted triangle, above Saudia titles in English (starboard) or Arabic (port). A grey or natural metal finish appears below the cheatline, which is delicately trimmed in white.

शाही नेपाल वायुसेवा
9N-ACA

sabena
F-GCBB

SCANDINAVIAN
SAS
SAS
OY-KDK
BOEING 767

saudia
HZ-AIM

SINGAPORE AIRLINES

The national airline of Singapore was created on January 28th 1972 to succeed the jointly operated Malaysia-Singapore Airlines-MSA. Operations were initiated on October 1st of that year and now connect Singapore with seventy international destinations, serving major cities in Africa, Europe, the Middle East, North America and the Asia-Pacific region. All-cargo services are also provided on a long-haul basis and since the introduction of a Boeing 737-300F in November 1992 to Bandar Seri Begawan, Bangkok, Dhaka, Ho Chi Minh City, Hong Kong, Madras and Phnom Penh regionally.

A modern fleet is standardised on Airbus Industrie and Boeing equipment and currently includes six A310-200s, sixteen A310-300s (plus one on order), one 737-300F freighter, four 747-200Bs (two leased out), four Boeing 747-200F freighters, fourteen 747-300s, twenty-four 747-400s and two 747-400Fs (plus four on order). The airline has also ordered seventeen A340-300s and twenty-three additional 747-400s for delivery between 1995 and 2003. The new aircraft will be used to replace 747-200s, 747-300s and some earlier 747-400s as part of the carrier's ongoing fleet renewal policy.

The livery illustrated by Boeing 747-412 'Megatop' 9V-SMF was introduced by Singapore Airlines in 1987, having been re-styled for the 1990s by its original creator - Walter Landor Associates of California. The design features foreshortened cheatlines of blue and gold, with the windows underscored by a narrow orange pinstripe. The tail motif remains as before, but with the stylised bird reproduced in gold (instead of yellow) and the trailing edge now sporting orange trim. Singapore Airlines titling is displayed on the cabin roof in blue upper-case lettering, accompanied by the national flag, with a reproduction of the tail motif appearing in miniature on each of the grey painted engine housings. The tail colouring is also mirrored on the winglets of relevant types, minus the bird motif.

SOBELAIR

Sobelair was created in July 1946 and is a wholly-owned subsidiary of the Belgian national carrier, Sabena. Inclusive-tour charters are flown from Brussels to holiday destinations in the Mediterranean, Africa, the Far East and Caribbean.

The carrier is equipped with a fleet of three Boeing 737-200s, one 737-300, three 737-400s and a wide-bodied Boeing 767-300/ER (leased from AWAS). The latter was delivered in June 1994 and operates long haul charters to Bangkok, Mombassa and the Caribbean. Additional aircraft are usually leased in during the peak summer months, but these rarely adopt Sobelair markings.

Sobelair's livery has always been identical to that worn by its parent company Sabena, with the two carrier's distinguished only by the titling displayed. In its latest form, illustrated by Boeing 737-229 OO-SBT, the Sobelair image is further compromised by the display of secondary Sabena titling in the standard pale blue tint.

SOUTH AFRICAN AIRWAYS

South African Airways was established by the Union Government on February 1st 1934 as a subsidiary of South African Railways to take over the assets of Union Airways, which had provided a small network of services between Cape Town, Port Elizabeth, Durban and Johannesburg. The new airline began operations on February 1st 1934 and by January 1946 its network reached as far as London (England). Today, intercontinental flights connect Johannesburg, Durban and Cape Town with Amsterdam, Athens, Bangkok, Dubai, Frankfurt, Hamburg, Hong Kong, Ilha do Sal, Larnaca, Lisbon, London, Manchester, Miami, Milan, Munich, New York, Paris, Perth, Rio de Janeiro, Singapore, Sydney, Taipei, Tel Aviv and Zurich The carrier also operates a domestic network of scheduled passenger and cargo services, together with regional flights.

The carrier employs a fleet of seven Airbus Industrie A320-200s, seven A300B2/B4s and fourteen Boeing 737-200s for domestic and regional operations, supplemented by the long haul fleet of five Boeing 747SPs (two leased out), six 747-200Bs, two 747-300s, four 747-400s and one 767-200/ER (with a second to be added in late 1994 - both via LAM Mozambique). Additional cargo capacity is provided by a converted A300C4 freighter and more locally by a small fleet of leased Antonov An-32s.

The carrier's livery is based on the national colours of orange, white and blue, and uses dual language titling to promote a bold South African identity. A bright orange tail provides the setting for the carrier's winged springbok motif, which is reproduced in blue with white edging. Blue and orange also combine to colour a bold 'straight through' cheatline arrangement, which underlines secondary blue titling and black initials - corresponding to the language (English-starboard, Afrikaanse-port). In its latest form, illustrated by Boeing 747-444 ZS-SAV, the cabin exterior is painted white overall.

SPANAIR

Spanair was created in 1986 and began operations in March 1988, operating passenger charters to points in Europe from Palma and the Canary Islands. Originally formed in association with SAS and now affiliated with Airtours, Spanair also operates long haul flights to points in the Caribbean, Mexico and the United States.

A modern fleet is currently standardised on SAS equipment and includes eleven McDonnell Douglas MD-83s and two Boeing 767-300/ERs, all of which are leased.

Spanair's livery, illustrated by Boeing 767-3Y0/ER EC-FHA, is based on the white exterior finish of SAS to enable aircraft to be transferred between the two carriers with the minimum of fuss. High visibility Spanair titling is displayed in dark blue across the forward cabin section, with the corporate motif adding a touch of colour to the fin and engine housings in the form of curvaceous orange and blue bands.

SINGAPORE AIRLINES
MEGATOP

sobelair
OO-SBT
CALEDONIAN

SOUTH AFRICAN AIRWAYS
SAA

Spanair
EC-FHA

SUDAN AIRWAYS

Sudan Airways was formed in 1947 and began domestic operations as a sudsidiary of the Sudan Railways System. International flights were added in 1954 and now connect the capital, Khartoum, with points in Africa, Asia, Europe and the Middle East. The carrier also operates a scheduled domestic network throughout the Sudan.

For domestic and regional operations Sudan Airways is equipped with three DHC-6 Twin Otter 300s, two Fokker 50s and two Boeing 737-200s. A single Airbus Industrie A320-200 is used on routes to Asmara, Cairo, Jeddah, Luqa, Rome and Sanaa, with two Airbus A310-300s and a newly acquired A300-600 providing additional capacity to Abu Dhabi, Amman, Cairo, Damascus, Doha, Dubai, Frankfurt, Jeddah, Kano, Karachi, London, Nairobi, Ndjamena, Paris, Riyadh and Sharjah.

The livery illustrated by Airbus Industrie A310-304 F-OGQN was introduced by Sudan Airways in July 1974. The obvious choice of sand yellow and Nile blue is very originally styled to sweep along the fuselage in a double step and culminate in black Sudan titling along the leading edge of the fin. The titling is reproduced in English on the starboard (right) side and Arabic on the other, and also appears in both languages over the forward cheatline arrangement, together with the corporate bird motif. The national flag is displayed alongside the forward passenger doors, with the cabin exterior and engine housings painted white.

SWISSAIR

Swissair was formed on March 26th 1931 by the amalgamation of Ad Astra Aero AG and Basler Luftverkehr (known as Balair), which had operated services to France and Germany since April 12th 1926. In the years that followed Swissair set many standards in European air travel, becoming the first airline to employ stewardesses (in 1933) and the first in Europe to introduce the Douglas DC-2 into service, which inaugurated the route between Zurich, Basle and London in 1935. Today, the airline connects Switzerland with points in Africa, Asia, the Middle and Far East and North and South America. An extensive domestic and inter-European network has been developed in association with Crossair, which is a 38%-owned regional subsidiary.

Swissair is currently equipped with a fleet of five Airbus Industrie A310-200s (leased from ILFC), five A310-300s, five Boeing 747-300s, ten Fokker 100s, twenty-four McDonnell Douglas MD-81s and thirteen MD-11s. However, between 1995 and 1997 the MD-80s and A310-200s will be phased out and replaced by a fleet of five A319-100s (leased from ILFC), sixteen A320-200s and eight A321-100s.

Swissair unveiled its latest livery on May 18th 1994 in a special ceremony involving Fokker 100 HB-IVH (illustrated). The new design is similar in style to that adopted by subsidiary Balair-CTA, but with the fuselage underside coloured in a lilac-tinted shade of grey instead of dark blue. The 'family' theme is extended to the style and application of red Swissair titles on the cabin roof, with the traditional Swiss tail motif remaining the focal point of the livery as before. Initially colouring two A310-300s and one Fokker 100, the new image will be phased in as part of the routine maintenance schedule and by twenty-nine Airbus narrow-bodies to be delivered between 1995 and 1997.

SYRIANAIR-SYRIAN ARAB AIRLINES

Syrianair was created on January 1st 1961 in partnership with United Arab Airlines and commenced domestic and regional operations in October of that year using three Douglas DC-6s supplied by the Egyptian carrier. Today, the company links Damascus with cities in Europe, North Africa and the Indian sub continent, with its domestic and regional network serving points throughout the Middle East, including Abu Dhabi, Aleppo, Bahrain, Beirut, Deirezzor, Dhahran, Doha, Dubai, Istanbul, Jeddah, Kameshli, Kuwait, Latakia, Riyadh, Sanaa, Sharjah and Tehran.

The carrier is equipped with a mixed fleet of western and 'Soviet' built types, with six Boeing 727-200s serving at the heart of its international operations, supplemented by two 747SPs, six Tupolev Tu-134B-3s and three Tu-154Ms. The Boeing 747SPs provide service to Bombay, Abu Dhabi, Delhi, Dhahran, Munich, Jeddah, Karachi, London, Paris and Sharjah; the Tu-154Ms serve Algiers, Cairo, Istanbul, Moscow, Riyadh and Tunis; and the Tu-134s connect Damascus with Budapest, Larnaca, Prague and Sofia, whilst also operating domestic and Government-VIP flights. Additional domestic capacity is provided by six Yakovlev Yak-40s and five Antonov An-26s, with four Ilyushin Il-76M freighters available for commercial or government/military use.

Syrianair uses a bright shade of Mediterranean blue to colour a trimmed cheatline arrangement, which is centred at window level and underlines similarly coloured Syrianair titling in both English and Arabic. An encircled tail motif is displayed in white on blue and appears in the form of a large mythical bird, with tail feathers outstretched - as illustrated by Ilyushin Il-76M YK-ATD. The fuselage is painted white down to wing level and grey thereafter, with the national flag displayed at the rear. Note: the Yak-40s and Antonov An-26s wear a separate 'domestic' livery.

TAP-AIR PORTUGAL

TAP-Air Portugal was formed by the Secretariate of Civil Aeronautics on March 14th 1945 and commenced regular scheduled operations on September 19th 1946, initially between Lisbon and Madrid. Several months after the inaugural flight a second regular service was opened to Lourenco Marques, linking Portugal with its major African colonies. Known as the 'Imperial Line', the service to six days to complete and routed via Casablanca, Villa Cisneros, Bathurst, Robertsville, Accra, Libreville, Luanda, Leopoldeville, Luluabourg, Elizabethville and Salisbury. Known as TAP-Air Portugal since 1979, the carrier now provides scheduled passenger and freight services to points in Africa, the Caribbean, Europe, the Middle East and North and South America, with domestic flights linking Lisbon with Faro, Funchal (Madeira), Ponta Delgada (Azores) and Porto. The operations of Air Atlantis, a former charter subsidiary, have also been absorbed.

The carrier currently employs a fleet of six Airbus Industrie A320-200s, five A310-300s, seven Boeing 737-200s, one 737-200C, nine 737-300s and seven Lockheed TriStar 500s (including one leased to TAAG Angola Airlines), with four A340-300s to be added between 1994 and 1996.

The livery illustrated by Lockheed TriStar-500 CS-TEG was introduced in 1979 to succeed the previous TAP Airline of Portugal image. The national colours of red and green are promoted on the fuselage and fin, the former as a bold cheatline starting at the nose and the latter as a downward extension of the red TAP tail motif - with the two merging at the rear. Air Portugal titling is displayed in black uppercase lettering on the cabin roof, accompanied by the national flag, with white colouring the fuselage down to wing level and grey or natural metal used below. Note: cheatlines appear below window level on all Airbus and Boeing types.

SUDAN
F-OGON

swissair
HB-IVH

SYRIAN AIR
IL-76M
YK-ATD

AIR PORTUGAL
CS-TEG

TAROM

Tarom was originally formed as a joint venture with the Soviet Government in 1946 under the name of TARS-Transporturi Aeriene Romana Sovietica to succeed the pre-war airline LARES, using a fleet of Lisunov Li-2s. The present title was adopted in 1954 when the company came under the full control of the Romanian Government. Scheduled passenger and freight services now link Bucharest with Abu Dhabi, Amman, Amsterdam, Athens, Bahrain, Bangkok, Beirut, Berlin, Brussels, Cairo, Calcutta, Chicago, Copenhagen, Damascas, Delhi, Dubai, Frankfurt, Istanbul, Karachi, Kuwait, Larnaca, London, Madrid, Moscow, New York, Paris, Prague, Rome, Sofia, Tehran, Tel Aviv, Thessaloniki, Vienna, Warsaw and Zurich. Domestic services and international charters are also undertaken.

A mixed fleet currently includes three Airbus Industrie A310-300s, sixteen Antonov An-24RVs (for domestic and regional services), thirteen British Aerospace/RomBac 1-11-500s, three Boeing 707-320Cs (two configured as freighters), five 737-300s, four Ilyushin Il-18D/Vs, three Il-62s and eight Tupolev Tu-154B-1/2s.

Most aircraft now wear the livery illustrated by Boeing 737-38J YR-BGB, which was first introduced in early 1991. A white cabin exterior provides a clean backdrop for blue Tarom titling, from which a similarly coloured pinstripe is formed. The blue and white combination is also used to colour the tail and stylised bird motif respectively, and again with the reproduction of a small motif on the engine housings - but with the colours reversed. All types have adopted the livery with the exception of the older Il-18s.

THAI AIRWAYS INTERNATIONAL

The flag-carrier of Thailand was formed in August 1954 to take over the international routes of Thai Airways, in co-operation with Scandinavian Airlines System-SAS. The airline has since absorbed the domestic operations of Thai Airways and now provides scheduled services linking Bangkok with forty-nine cities throughout Asia, Australasia, Europe, the Middle and Far East and North America, as well as sixteen points within Thailand.

For domestic and regional operations the carrier is equipped with two ATR42-300s, two ATR72-200s, two Airbus Industrie A310-200s, eleven A300B4s, one A300C4, six A300-600s, ten A300-600Rs and seven Boeing 737-400s. Additional capacity is provided by six 747-200Bs, two 747-300s, eight 747-400s and four McDonnell Douglas MD-11s - the latter used exclusively on services to Australia and New Zealand, and to Brussels and Zurich in Europe. Long haul destinations served by the 747 fleet include Athens, Frankfurt, London, Los Angeles, Madrid, Paris, Rome and Stockholm. The airline has ordered eight A330-300s for delivery between 1994 and 1995 and eight 777-200s for delivery between 1996 and 1998. Three Boeing 737-200s have been leased out to other carriers, and five British Aerospace 146-300s and three McDonnell Douglas DC-10-30s are currently awaiting disposal.

The livery illustrated by Boeing 747-4D7 HS-TGH was introduced by Thai Airways International in 1975, having been designed by Walter Landor Associates under a brief which called for a reflection of the rich heritage of Thailand in both colour and form. A vast Royal Orchid motif fills the tail in shades of magenta, gold and purple, and is repeated on the forward fuselage as the starting point for a similarly coloured cheatline. The fuselage and fin is painted white overall, with abbreviated Thai lettering displayed on the cabin roof in purple.

TMA-TRANS MEDITERRANEAN AIRWAYS

Trans Mediterranean Airways was formed in 1953 and commenced operations using two Avro York freighters on non-scheduled services, flying fresh produce to oil stations in the Arabian Gulf. On February 12th 1959 it became a joint stock company and obtained Lebanese Government approval to operate regular scheduled freight services. These are now flown from various points in the Middle East to freight terminals in Europe, South East Asia, the Far East and the United States. Scheduled cargo services are also operated on behalf of Kuwait Airways.

TMA was one of the first all-cargo airlines to introduce Boeing 747 freighters, but years of internal unrest in the Lebanon have left the carrier with a modest fleet of six Boeing 707-320Cs - of which three are usually assigned to the Kuwait Airways contract.

Many of TMA's Boeing 707s have displayed colourful liveries throughout their flying careers, having earlier served with Braniff International of the United States. It was infact the introduction of these ex-Braniff aircraft that inspired the current TMA livery, illustrated by Boeing 707-327C OD-AFY. A bright yellow tail displays the corporate motif of a yellow triangle, with green TMA initials underlined by black wings, appearing within a green spherical enclosure. A green cabin exterior is violated only by the registration markings and TMA of Lebanon titling in yellow, with the national flag placed above the tail motif.

TOWER AIR

Tower Air was formed in 1982 when Tower Travel, a charter company specialising in travel between New York and Israel, purchased the fleet and assets of a Flying Tigers subsidiary known as Metro International. Today, the airline operates scheduled low fare scheduled services connecting New York with Los Angeles, Miami, Orlando, San Francisco and San Juan (Puerto Rico) domestically; with Amsterdam, Dublin, Paris and Shannon in Europe; and New Delhi (India); Tel Aviv (Israel) and Sao Paulo (Brasil). Scheduled service is also provided between Los Angeles and Miami, and the carrier has applied for authority to connect New York with London-Stansted. Contract and ad-hoc charters are also flown, including flights for the U.S. military.

The fleet is standardised on Boeing 747-100 and -200 series aircraft, of which thirteen are currently operated (including two in all-cargo configuration).

The livery illustrated by Boeing 747-131 N608FF was introduced by Tower Air during the summer of 1991. A blue coloured underside, trimmed above in orange, sweeps over the upper rear fuselage and bleeds off the fin's trailing edge, lining blue Tower Air titling on both the forward cabin and fin. The letter 'A' forms a blue and orange corporate motif, which is also repeated in miniature on white painted engine housings.

YR-BGB
TAROM

Thai

TMA OF LEBANON
OD-AFY

Tower Air
Tower Air

TRANSAERO

Transaero was formed in 1990 and is known to provide scheduled passenger services connecting Moscow-Sheremetyevo with Almaty (Kazakhstan), Kiev (Ukraine), Minsk (Belorussia), Norilsk and Sochi (Russian Federation), Riga (Latvia), Tashkent (Uzbekistan) and Tel Aviv in Israel. International passenger and freight charters are flown to points in the Middle and Near East, with freight charters also serving western Europe.

The airline is equipped with three Boeing 737-200s, two 757-200s (leased from the GPA Group), one Ilyushin Il-76M (freighter), two Il-86s and one Tupolev Tu-154S (freighter).

Based on the Russian flag colours of blue, white and red, the livery adopted by Transaero is similar in many respects to that of Air France, in terms of both style and colouring. Both liveries are based on a white exterior finish, with titles displayed in blue uppercase lettering on the forward cabin roof. However, in this instance the titling is dissected by a white pinstripe and appears alongside a small Russian flag, as illustrated by Ilyushin Il-86 RA-86123. The tail markings are made to look visually similar by their colouring and pinstriping, but are infact totally different. In the case of Transaero, the motif is arrow-shaped and the values of colour are equal, whereas the Air France application is diagonal and predominantly blue.

TRANSAVIA AIRLINES

Transavia Airlines was formed in 1965 and began charter and inclusive tour operations on November 17th 1966 when the Dutch Dancing Theatre was flown to Naples. Previously known as Transavia (Limburg) NV and later Transavia Holland (between 1967 and 1986), the carrier now also provides scheduled passenger services linking Amsterdam-Schiphol with Alicante, Faro, Funchal, Gran Canaria, Heraklion, London, Malaga, Malta, Palma de Mallorca and Tenerife, and has been 80% owned by KLM since 1991.

An all-Boeing fleet currently includes six Boeing 737-200s, eight 737-300s and three 757-200s. The 737-300 fleet is increased to nine aircraft during the summer season and reduced to six during the winter under a seasonal interchange agreement with TAESA of Mexico. Transavia Airlines has ordered four additional 757-200s for delivery between 1995 and 1997.

The livery illustrated by Boeing 737-2K2 PH-TVP was introduced in its original form in February 1986 and revised exactly six years later to feature a single green shade. The design is based on a series of pinstriped cheatlines, which emanate from a white 'T' initial on the forward fuselage . Transavia titles are displayed parallel to the fin's leading edge, with green lowercase lettering partly enclosed by a black outlined 'T'. Secondary titles also appear on the engine housings, with the Dutch flag confirming the airline's nationality on the forward cabin roof.

TUNIS AIR

Tunis Air was formed in 1948 as a branch of Air France, with the participation of the Tunisian Government and other private interests. Operations began in 1949 over a small local network and were soon extended to Casablanca, Tripoli and Ghadames - a vital oasis on the borders of Libya, Tunisia and Algeria. Services to Europe were inaugurated in 1953 and now connect Tunisia with twenty-eight cities in fourteen countries, including eight in France and five in Germany. Regional services are flown to Abu Dhabi, Algiers, Cairo, Casablanca, Dakar, Damascus, Jeddah and Nouakchott, with Tunis and Monastir linked domestically. Although most flights originate from the capital, Tunis, the carrier also flies from Djerba, Monastir, Sfax, Tabarka and Tozeur.

Tunis Air is currently equipped with eight Airbus Industrie A320-200s, seven Boeing 727-200s, four 737-200s and three 737-500s, with a wide-bodied A300B4 used on trunk routes to Casablanca, Istanbul, Jeddah, Nice, Paris and Rome. Additional capacity is leased-in for the summer season, usually from Air Atlanta of Iceland.

The traditional leaping gazelle motif of Tunis Air was given a new staring role with the introduction of the carrier's first Airbus Industrie A320-211 in October 1990. Previously embraced by red TA initials, the gazelle now appears ahead of extended pinstripes in the national colours of red and white, which rise from the lower rear fuselage to create a leaping effect. A white cabin exterior promotes Tunisair titling in red uppercase lettering, alongside its Arabic equivalent, with the national flag displayed at the rear. The gazelle motif is also reproduced on the engine housings in its more usual horizontal position.

TURKMENISTAN AIRLINES

Turkmenistan Airlines, formerly Aeroflot-Turkmenistan Directorate, is the name under which several regional divisions collectively provide air services within the state of Turkmenistan. The largest of these is based in the capital, Ashkhabad, and provides international passenger and freight services throughout the region, serving points in the Indian sub-continent and the Middle and Near East, as well as Moscow and other cities within the CIS. Passenger services to Europe, possibly via Ankara or Istanbul, are also planned. Other divisions are based at Chardzhou and Krasnovodsk, which are among the many cities served domestically.

The carrier is known to have inherited a fleet of twenty-two Antonov An-24s (various models), five An-26s, twelve Tupolev Tu-154B-1/B-2s and ten Yakovlev Yak-40s, and has since added three Boeing 737-300s, four Yak-42Ds (six more on order) and five Ilyushin Il-76TD freighters. A VIP-configured Boeing 757 is operated on behalf of the Presidential Flight, having been delivered new in December 1993.

Boeing 737-341 EZ-A001 illustrates the definative livery of Turkmenistan Airlines, introduced with the delivery of this aircraft in November 1992 and since applied to other 737s and the Presidential 757. In its complete form, the design is based on a white exterior finish with two-tone blue cheatlines applied below window level. The darker shade is also used to colour Turkmenistan titling, appearing alongside the national flag on the cabin roof, and a spherical tail motif accommodating a stylised white bird. Other types display a similar livery based on the blue coloured cheatline of Aeroflot.

TRANSAERO
RA-86123

Transavia
PH-TVP

TUNISAIR
TUNISAIR
الخطوط التونسية

Turkmenistan
EZ-A001
BOEING 737-300

TURKISH AIRLINES

Turkish Airlines was set up under the Ministry of National Defence on May 20th 1933 and was known as Devlet Hava Yollari (Turkish State Airlines) until February 20th 1956, when the airline became an independent corporation. It initially concentrated on establishing domestic links, but international expansion began in 1947 with the opening of a route to Athens, followed in 1950 by services to Nicosia, Beirut and Cairo. International services are now offered from Ankara, Istanbul, Antalya, Izmir and Adana to points in Europe, the Middle and Far East, North Africa and the United States. An extensive domestic route system is also maintained.

The carrier is equipped with a fleet of eight Airbus Industrie A310-200s, seven A310-300s, three A340-300s (plus two on order), eight Avroliner RJ-100s, ten Boeing 727-200s, twenty-five 737-400s (four more to be acquired in 1995) and two 737-500s. Nine McDonnell Douglas DC-9-30s have now been parked, awaiting disposal. Additional cargo capacity is provided by leased Antonov An-12 and McDonnell Douglas DC-8-70F equipment.

The current Turkish Airlines livery projects a bold national identity in using the flag colours of red and white, with blue Turkish lettering displayed on the cabin roof, preceded by the national flag. Illustrated by Airbus Industrie A340-311 TC-JDJ, the design is based on a white cabin exterior and red painted fin. The tail motif appears within a white spherical enclosure and signifies flight in the form of a stylised red bird.

TWA-TRANS WORLD AIRLINES

TWA's history goes back to 1925 when the first of its parental foursome, Western Air Express, bid for a mail contract covering the Los Angeles-Salt Lake City route, the first service being inaugurated on April 17th 1926. Transcontinental and Western Air was formed on October 1st 1930 through a merger of a part of Western Air Express (the other part became Western Airlines), TAT-Maddux and Pittsburgh Aviation Industries, with the present name being adopted in May 1950. TWA developed its domestic trunk routes and was instrumental in the design of such famous aircraft as the Douglas DC-1, DC-2, DC-3, the Boeing Stratoliner and the Lockheed Constellation, with which the airline inaugurated its first overseas flight (from Washington to Paris) on December 5th 1945. Today, the carrier operates to over one hundred domestic destinations with main traffic hubs situated at New York and St. Louis, and internationally to points in Europe, North Africa and the Middle East.

A vast fleet currently includes around fifty Boeing 727-200s, ten 747-100s, two 747-200Bs, ten 767-200/ERs, three 767-300/ERs, twenty-one Lockheed TriStars (various models), seven McDonnell Douglas DC-9-10s, thirty-six DC-9-30s, three DC-9-40s, twelve DC-9-50s, around thirty MD-82s and twelve MD-83s. Ten Airbus Industrie A330-300s have been ordered for delivery in 1997.

The livery illustrated by Boeing 767-231/ER N601TW was unveiled in its original form on November 30th 1974. Using the traditional corporate colours of red and white, the design centres on a dart-shaped cheatline arrangement, which proceeds below window level before ultimately embracing the lower rear fuselage. Trans World titling is displayed in red uppercase lettering, with a white TWA motif reversed out of a red parallelogram on the fin.

UNITED AIRLINES

United Airlines was formed on July 31st 1931 as the management company for Boeing Air Transport, National Air Transport, Pacific Air Transport and Varney Air Lines, and became operational on July 20th 1934. Building on the existing routes of its predecessors, United established a comprehensive coast-to-coast network, which was extended to Hawaii in 1947. One of the most significant developments in the airline's post war history was the purchase, on June 1st 1961, of Capital Airlines, in what was at the time the biggest ever airline merger. In addition to a comprehensive domestic route structure, with major traffic hubs at Chicago (O'Hare), Denver, San Francisco and Washington, United Airlines also serves points in the Asia-Pacific region, Canada, the Caribbean, Europe and Central and South America. Additional domestic coverage is provided by several United Express regional partner airlines.

The carrier employs one of the world's largest fleets of aircraft which, despite its size, has also been extensively modernised in recent times. One hundred Boeing 737-300s, sixty-one 737-500s, eighty-eight 757-200s, twenty-four 747-400s and twenty-three 767-300/ERs have been phased in to date, with deliveries of fifty ordered Airbus Industrie A320-200s currently in progress. A further thirty-seven 737s, fifteen 747-400s, thirty 777-200s and four 777-200/ERs are on order. These continue to be supplemented by over ninety 727-200s, sixty-nine 737-200s, eighteen 747-100s, nine 747-200s, ten 747SPs (now stored), nineteen 767-200s, forty-four McDonnell Douglas DC-10-10s (some stored) and eight DC-10-30s.

The livery illustrated by Boeing 747-122 N4729U was introduced by United Airlines in January 1993. Designed by Walter Landor Associates, its features all-encompassing shades of dark blue and grey with titles and other lettering in white. Remnants of the previous livery appear in the form of a narrow orange, red and blue cheatline and the familiar double 'U' tail motif, the latter displayed over horizontal bands of medium and dark blue.

USAIR

USAir was formed on March 5th 1937 as All-American Aviation and commenced operations from Pittsburgh on September 13th of that year. The name Allegheny Airlines was adopted in 1953 and mergers with Lake Central Airlines (1968) and Mohawk Airlines (1972) greatly expanded the Allegheny route system, with the present name being adopted on October 28th 1979. Transatlantic operations were introduced on August 5th 1989 following a merger with Piedmont Airlines, serving points in France, Germany and the United Kingdom. An extensive domestic network extends regionally to points in Canada and the Caribbean. Regional subsidiaries include Allegheny Commuter, Henson Aviation and Jetstream Intl., with these being among the many airlines now operating under the USAir Express banner. Services connecting Baltimore and Pittsburgh with London-Gatwick are flown in conjunction with British Airways, which has been partnered with USAir since January 21st 1993.

A vast domestic and regional fleet currently includes twenty-seven Boeing 727-200s, eighty-one 737-200s, one hundred and one 737-300s, fifty-four 737-400s, twenty-six 757-200s (plus fifteen more on order), seventeen Fokker F.28-1000s (most now stored), twenty-four F.28-4000s (some stored), forty Fokker 100s, seventy-three McDonnell Douglas DC-9-30s and thirty-one MD-81/82s. Additional domestic capacity is also provided by the long-haul fleet of thirteen Boeing 767-200/ERs, two of which are operated in British Airways markings.

USAir's livery, illustrated by Boeing 767-201/ER N648US, combines the dark blue and red colouring of Allegheny Airlines with the bright red and pale blue shades of Piedmont Airlines, having been introduced following the USAir-Piedmont merger in 1989. The natural metal fuselage finish originates from the previous USAir livery and is dissected by a bold red cheatline, trimmed above in blue. USAir titling is displayed in white on a blue coloured fin, between horizontal bands of red, and also on the cabin roof in bright red and pale blue respectively, outlined in white.

TURKISH
AIRBUS A340

TWA
TRANS WORLD

UNITED AIRLINES

USAir
USAir

UZBEKISTAN AIRWAYS

Uzbekistan Airways was formed in 1992 to succeed a former Aeroflot Directorate based in the capital, Tashkent. Scheduled passenger services are currently flown to points in Asia, Europe, and the Middle and Far East, including Almaty (Kazakhstan); Dnepropetrovsk, Kiev, Lvov and Simferopol (Ukraine); Khabarovsk, Krasnodar, Mineralnye Vody, Novosibirsk, Omsk, St. Petersburg and Sochi (Russian Federation); Delhi, Istanbul, Jeddah, Karachi, Kuala Lumpur, London, Sharjah, Tel Aviv and Urumqi (China). Services to New York (via Manchester, England) are also planned. Domestic services are also operated from Tashkent and Samarkland under the local name of Uzbekistan Havo Jullary, with international cargo charters also undertaken.

The carrier is currently known to operate two Antonov An-12 freighters, twenty-three An-24s, four Ilyushin Il-62s, ten Il-62Ms, sixteen Il-76TD freighters, ten Il-86s, two Il-114s, twenty-five Tupolev Tu-154s (all models) and twenty-eight Yakovlev Yak-40s. Two Airbus Industrie A310-300s were added in mid-1993 and have replaced Il-62Ms on select international routes.

The featured livery is synonymous to the flagship A310-300s and was created by the manufacturer in the image of the Presidential fleet. In this instance, the stylised swan motif is displayed in green on a yellow sphere, but more widely appears in white on a blue painted fin. On the Airbus aircraft the blue and green fuselage colouring is guided by narrow red pinstripes (based on the national flag), with Uzbekistan titles displayed in black uppercase lettering below the forward cabin windows. On other types the titling is blue and appears above or below a blue and green cheatline arrangement, with the blue line flaring to colour the upper rear fuselage and fin. A separate domestic division, operating as Uzbekistan Havo Jullary, uses yet another variation, not to mention to many aircraft that continue to be operated in basic Aeroflot markings.

VARIG

Varig was organised with Brasilian capital on May 7th 1927 and began operations on February 3rd 1928 on the Porto Alegre-Rio Grande, taken over from the Kondor Syndikat. In 1951 Varig acquired Aerea Geral, a domestic operator, and then became the largest airline in South America in August 1961 when it took over the REAL consortium and its fleet and routes. On February 9th 1965 the international routes of Panair do Brasil were transferred to Varig, and in May 1975 a controlling interest was acquired in Cruzeiro - which has since been completely absorbed. Varig now serves forty-five points within Brasil, with international routes connecting Rio de Janeiro and Sao Paulo with Amsterdam, Barcelona, Copenhagen, Frankfurt, Lisbon, London, Madrid, Milan, Oporto, Paris, Rome and Zurich in Europe; Chicago, Los Angeles, Mexico City, Miami, New York and San Francisco in North America; Cape Town, Johannesburg, Lagos, Luanda and Sal Island in Africa; and several major cities throughout Central and South America.

Varig is equipped with five Boeing 727-100F freighters, seventeen 737-200s, twenty-six 737-300s (all leased), three 747-200Bs, three 747-300s, six 767-200/ERs, three 767-300/ERs, ten McDonnell Douglas DC-10-30s and six MD-11s. Three 747-400s have now been returned to ILFC, although six have been ordered for delivery between 1995 and 1998. Eleven 737-300s are due to be delivered between 1994 and 1997, possibly to replace leased aircraft.

With bright yellow, green and blue national colours at its disposal, it is perhaps strange that Varig should remain loyal to the sombre blue image that has now coloured its fleet for several decades. A bold blue cheatline curves under the cockpit windows and is dissected at window level by two narrow white pinstripes. Varig titles are displayed in expanded blue lettering on the cabin roof and repeated in black below the classic compass motif on the fin, with the national identity confirmed by a small Brasilian flag and black Brasil wording above the forward cheatline. A traditional flying figurehead motif is positioned near the forward passenger door, as illustrated by Boeing 767-241/ER PP-VNP.

VIASA - VENEZUELAN INTERNATIONAL AIRWAYS

Viasa was formed in 1961 to take over the international routes operated by Avensa and LAV, and today operates scheduled passenger and freight services connecting Caracas with Amsterdam, Athens, Frankfurt, Lisbon, London, Madrid, Milan, Paris, Porto, Rome, Santiago de Compostela and Zurich in Europe; Houston, Miami, New York and Toronto in North America; Bogota, Buenos Aires, Lima, Quito, Rio de Janeiro, San Jose, Santiago and Sao Paulo in Central and South America; Aruba, Curacao, Havana and Santo Domingo in the Caribbean; and Barcelona, Maracaibo, Porlamar and Puerto Ordaz domestically. Viasa is now associated with Iberia of Spain.

The carrier's regional network is served by five Boeing 727-200s (ex-Iberia) and two Airbus Industrie A300B4s, with five McDonnell Douglas DC-10-30s providing additional capacity and range.

Viasa uses a combination of bright orange and blue in a livery which is both colourful and distinctive. The focal point of the design is unquestionably the orange painted fin, which provides a solid backdrop for white Viasa titling and also accommodates a token national flag. A narrow cheatline arrangement starts at the nose and proceeds below window level to the rear, separating the white upper and grey lower fuselage colouring in two values of blue. Viasa titling, offset by horizontal extensions formed by the letter 'S', is also reproduced in orange on the forward cabin roof and balanced by blue Venezuela lettering at the rear.

VIRGIN ATLANTIC AIRWAYS

Virgin Atlantic Airways was formed in June 1984 to offer low fare scheduled passenger services between London-Gatwick and New York-Newark. A feeder service was later added to connect Maastricht in Holland with the London end of the transatlantic service, but has since been discontinued. The carrier's scheduled network now connects London (Gatwick and Heathrow) with Boston, Hong Kong, Los Angeles, Miami, New York, Orlando and Tokyo. Services are also offered between London City and Dublin and London-Gatwick and Athens in association with CityJet and Southeast European Airlines respectively.

A fleet standardised on widebodied aircraft currently includes three Airbus Industrie A340-300s, one Boeing 747-100, seven 747-200Bs and one 747-400 (leased from ILFC). A fourth A340-300 and a second Boeing 747-400 should be in service by November 1994, possibly releasing some of the earlier 747s from the fleet. The airline has also contracted to lease a third 747-400 and one Airbus Industrie A340-300 from ILFC, for delivery in April and November 1996 respectively.

The current Virgin Atlantic livery was introduced by the airline's first A340-300 in November 1993. Based on a white cabin exterior, the design features red painted engine housings and matching tail colouring, with the Virgin signature reproduced in white. In its latest form, illustrated by Boeing 747-4Q8 G-VFAB, the livery also includes silver-coloured Virgin Atlantic titling - which is expected to be adopted fleetwide. A touch of glamour is provided by the curvaceous 'Virgin Lady' motif, which appears below the cockpit windows in a classic World War Two art form.

UZBEKISTAN
F-OGOY

BRASIL
VARIG
VARIG
VNP

VIASA
VIASA

Virgin
virgin atlantic

VIVA AIR

Viva Air was formed on February 24th 1988 as a joint venture between Iberia and Lufthansa to operate holiday charter flights from a base at Palma de Mallorca. Now 98% owned by Iberia, the carrier has since developed a scheduled international passenger network connecting Alicante, Barcelona, Madrid, Malaga and Palma de Mallorca with points throughout Europe and North Africa, with Barcelona also linked with Tel Aviv in Israel.

The airline currently operates nine Boeing 737-300s and has contracted to lease four additional aircraft from ILFC for delivery between March 1995 and April 1996.

Viva Air's livery was designed for the leisure market and reflects sun, sea and sand in an abstract form. Illustrated by Boeing 737-36E EC-FHR, the design is based on a white exterior finish with titles displayed on the lower forward fuselage in a combination of black, blue, red, green and yellow. The tail motif projects a warm and friendly image whilst also offering a clue to the airline's nationality, which is confirmed by a small Spanish flag displayed alongside the registration markings.

VNUKOVO AIRLINES

Vnukovo Airlines has replaced a former Aeroflot division in providing scheduled domestic services from Moscow-Vnukovo airport to points throughout the Russian Federation. The carrier is also known to serve Shevchenko (Kazakhstan) and other cities within the Commonwealth of Independent States, with international 'shopping' charters operated to Alexandria, Dubai, Istanbul and Sharjah on a regular basis. Vnukovo Airlines has developed a close working relationship with Greenair of Turkey and supplies aircraft and crews as and when required.

The carrier is known to operate no less than thirty-eight Tupolev Tu-154s (various models) and twenty-two Ilyushin Il-86s. Three Tu-204s have also been delivered to date.

The livery illustrated by Ilyushin Il-86 RA-86006 was introduced by Vnukovo Airlines in early 1994 to replace the previous Aeroflot image and is now progressively being adopted by all members of the fleet. Inverted bands of blue and gold are displayed at the forward and rear ends of the fuselage, which is painted white down to wing level and grey thereafter, with expanded Vnukovo Airlines titling appearing on the cabin roof in blue upper case lettering - in English on the starboard (right) side and Russian on the port (left) side. A solid blue tail band promotes stylised 'VA' initials in white, with the Russian flag promoted on the forward cabin roof.

WORLD AIRWAYS

World Airways was formed in 1948 and commenced operations that same year using two Curtiss C-46 Commandos. The airline's initial business consisted mostly of military contract work, although some commercial charter flights were also undertaken on an ad-hoc basis. From these humble beginnings, World Airways went on to become one of the world's leading passenger and freight charter airlines, expanding into the scheduled low fare passenger market from April 1979. Since September 1986, the carrier has focused on domestic and worldwide cargo charters and military and commercial contract work, the latter mostly on behalf of Garuda and Malaysia Airlines. World Airways re-started civil passenger operations in March 1993 and more recently applied for authority to operate scheduled flights connecting New York with Tel Aviv, Johannesburg and Cape Town. Passenger and cargo charters are now also offered from Miami to points in Europe, Latin America and Africa.

A well-equipped fleet is made up of four McDonnell Douglas DC-10-30CFs (one in passenger configuration), three MD-11s, one MD-11F freighter and two MD-11CFs (passenger or freight).

Due to its seasonal leasing commitments, World Airways now employs a more practical image that can be easily adapted for carriers such as Garuda or Malaysia Airlines when the need arises. The low profile design, illustrated by McDonnell Douglas MD-11 N271WA, simply promotes World titling in blue uppercase lettering on a fuselage that is painted white down to wing level and left natural metal below. The tail motif, which also forms the letter 'o' of the titles and features on the winglets of the MD-11s, is in the form of a blue coloured globe with lines of latitude and longitude reproduced in white.

ZAMBIA AIRWAYS

Zambia Airways was formed in 1963 as a subsidiary of the Central African Airways Corporation to take over that company's operations in the newly independent state of Zambia (formerly known as Northern Rhodesia). Operations began on July 1st 1964 over a domestic network and were extended to neighbouring countries four years later. Today, the carrier's international network reaches Bombay, Dar-es-Salaam, Gaborone, Harare, Johannesburg, Lilongwe, London and Nairobi. Scheduled domestic services are flown from the capital, Lusaka, to Ndola in the copperbelt region, Mansa, Kasama and Kasaba Bay in the Sumbu National Park and Lake Tanganyika areas, Mfuwe and Chipata in the Luangwa Valley and Livingstone by the spectacular Victoria Falls.

For domestic and regional operations Zambia Airways is equipped with two ATR42-300s and two Boeing 737-200s, with a single McDonnell Douglas DC-10-30 providing additional capacity on services to Bombay, Johannesburg and London.

The livery illustrated by McDonnell Douglas DC-10-30 N3016Z was introduced by Zambia Airways in March 1975. A quadruple cheatline arrangement is based on the national colours of green, red, black and orange, representing the fertile country, the blood of the people, the colour of the people and copper (the country's main export) respectively. The leading line ultimately fans out to colour the upper rear fuselage and fin in green, which provides the setting for an orange coloured eagle motif - reproduced in the form of an enclosed letter 'Z' The cheatline also separates the cabin colours of white and grey and underlines black Zambia Airways titling on the forward cabin roof, preceded by the national flag.

viva air
EC-FHR
air europa

VNUKOVO AIRLINES
RA-86008
IL-86

WORLD

Zambia Airways

INDEX